Ramadan
Reflections

T0322367

Ramadan Reflections

A guided journal

30 days of healing from the past,
journeying with presence and looking
ahead to an akhirah-focused future

ALIYAH UMM RAIYAAN

RIDER

10

Rider, an imprint of Ebury Publishing,
20 Vauxhall Bridge Road,
London SW1V 2SA

Rider is part of the Penguin Random House group of companies
whose addresses can be found at global.penguinrandomhouse.com

Penguin
Random House
UK

First published by Rider in 2023
www.penguin.co.uk

A CIP catalogue record for this book is available from the British Library

ISBN 9781846047633

Printed and bound in Great Britain by Clays Ltd, Elcograf S.p.A.

The authorised representative in the EEA is Penguin Random House Ireland,
Morrison Chambers, 32 Nassau Street, Dublin D02 YH68

Penguin Random House is committed to a sustainable future for our business, our readers
and our planet. This book is made from Forest Stewardship Council® certified paper

CONTENTS

PART 3:

PLANNING AND MOVING INTO AN AKHIRAH-FOCUSED
FUTURE 183

Introduction

Ramadan is one of the most sacred, most spiritual intimate months of the Islamic year. It is a month that teaches us so much about ourselves and our relationship to others, and nurtures the most important relationship of all – between us and our Lord, Allah (ﷻ subhanahu wa ta'ala – Glorious and Most High is He).

Allah 'azza wa jal (Glory be to Him) has made it clear that this is a month to break away from the norm, to do things differently in order to attain taqwa – a state of being consciously aware of Him.

Becoming conscious of Allah changes a person both inwardly and outwardly. The heart softens, the mind's thoughts develop an akhirah (eternal life)-focused clarity and the body submits and worships its Lord with deep devotion and love.

Ramadan Reflections is a journey within a journey. Divided into three parts, it encourages you to pay attention to the lessons of your past. It invites you to live mindfully and with presence in your present. It will assist you in planning an akhirah-focused future. Each part contains ten chapters, with each chapter representing one day of Ramadan. The chapter themes relate to my own faith and life as well as the lives of others. At the end of each chapter, you will find practical exercises designed to help you take what you have read deep within yourself so that this may manifest into actions loved by your Lord. 'Let Your Heart Ponder' is an invitation to be still, with powerful words that will focus your heart and thoughts. 'Du'a Invitation' is an opportunity for you to move your focused heart to speak to your Lord in sincere supplication. The 'Journal' sections include invitations to reflect upon particular themes and subjects, as well as to pen your personal thoughts in response to intimate journal prompts. At the end of each chapter, you are provided further space in which to write down your own reflections on the theme of the day and to allow for spiritual transformation to emerge.

Islamic terminology is translated in the first instance that it appears and a glossary for reference thereafter can be found at the back of the book. The term 'revert' refers to an individual who has converted to Islam. 'Revert' is used because it is the Islamic belief that everyone is born upon fitrah (the natural inclination to worship one Creator) and so those of us who become Muslim are simply reverting to that natural state.

On your very first reading of Ramadan Reflections, I encourage you to turn to each chapter on its designated day of Ramadan in chronological order. Yes, that means holding out until Day 1 of Ramadan before starting to work with this book! The Qur'an was revealed gradually so that we may internalise its messages slowly, with meaning. We are Muslim and human too. There is much benefit in slowing down on this journey to our Lord. Afterwards, on any subsequent readings of the book, I encourage you to dip in and out throughout the year depending on the needs of your heart and soul.

I also invite you to start each chapter with Bismillah (in the Name of Allah) and ask Al-Mujeeb, the One who responds to our du'a (personal prayer of supplication), to guide your mind and heart to take from it that which your soul specifically needs.

Our goal in the month of Ramadan is the same, and though readers of this book will read the same words on these pages, we all have a unique journey to the Lord of the Heavens and Earth. My du'a for you is that you are guided to a reading where Allah brings individualised meaning and lessons just for you.

There is a beautiful piece of writing by an unknown author that I came across many years ago. It describes the journey that you will undertake in this book. It reads:

Oh Allah,

I told You, I'm in pain. You said: 'Do not despair of the mercy of Allah.' (39:53)

I told You, Nobody knows what is in my heart. You said: 'Verily in the remembrance of Allah do hearts find rest.' (13:28)

I told You, Many people hurt me. You said: 'So pardon them and ask for forgiveness for them.' (3:159)

I told You, I feel I'm alone. You said: 'We are closer to him than his jugular vein.' (50:16)

I told You, my sins are so many. You said: 'And who can forgive sins except Allah.' (3:135)

I told You, Do not leave me. You said: 'So remember me, I will remember you.' (2:152)

I told You, I'm facing a lot of difficulties in life. You said: 'And whoever is conscious of Allah, He will make for him a way out.' (65:2)

I told You, I have dreams that I want to come true. You said: 'Call upon me, I will respond to you.' (40:60)

As we welcome the blessed month of Ramadan into our lives, I invite you to also welcome the thirty-day journey you will undertake with this book. This is your journal for this Ramadan. It is yours – interact with it as you wish. Highlight, underline and add your own notes if something resonates. This is all about you, your life and your journey to Allah ('azza wa jal).

I start this journey with the beautiful words of the scholar Ibn al-Qayyim who said,

In the heart of every human being, there is a sense of scattering which can only be gathered by turning to

Allah. And in the heart there is a sense of loneliness which can only be overcome by feeling the intimate nearness to Allah in solitude. And in the heart there is sadness which can only be removed by the joy of knowing Him and being true in worshipping Him. And in the heart there is anxiety which can only be put at ease by gathering one's self for Him and escaping from Him to Him.

Ibn al-Qayyim, *Madaarij As-Salikeen*

By Allah, for Allah and with Allah.

Let the journey begin.

Aliyah Umm Raiyaan

PART 1:

Healing and Taking Lessons from the Past

The famous companion of Muhammad (ﷺ) Umar bin al-Khattab (may Allah be pleased with him) was a drinker of alcohol who became Amir al-Mumineen, the Leader of the Believers.

Life is a story of many chapters, one bad chapter does not shape the end of the story.

Dear reader, I invite you to heal from your past.

DAY 1

Reflection

On 21 June 1999, I embraced Islam. Every year, I make it a ritual to pause and reflect on the year gone by. On my twenty-second year of being a Muslim, I took myself to a local park with a photograph. I reflected and wrote the following:

Today I have been a Muslim for twenty-two years.

This picture was a 22-years younger me. I was a new Muslim and embraced Islam from a rational conviction that Islam was the way of life prescribed by the Creator of the Heavens and the Earth, who is One with no partners; who sent down prophets and messengers with Muhammad (ﷺ) as His last and final messenger.

I look at this picture of me – of her, and a mixture of emotions envelop me. The innocence and the naivety. She embraced Islam with a pure heart and was convinced life would become easier now that she had found the truth. Little did she know then that it would be a journey of many trials.

There's so much I would tell her now.

I would tell her: slow down, take your time, study, learn, be and act authentically. The Qur'an was revealed gradually so that human hearts could absorb it and accept. So too must your journey be travelled gradually, as you are human as well as a Muslim.

I would tell her: the transition from disbelief to belief is a delicate one. It is not linear. It does not take place immediately upon the declaration of faith – the Shahaadah (declaration of faith) is simply the beginning of a fragile journey. A journey which requires a great deal of self-compassion, patience and self-love.

I would tell her: the love you need is the love of Allah first. The love of humans: sisters, husband, even your own children – they are all secondary.

I would tell her: focus on building your faith inwardly first as that is what will get you through the tough times and oh my, there will be many! Your hijab and the ability to form new foreign Arabic words are all surface-level changes. The real change that is required is that of reliance on Allah, patience, humility and a heart in constant dialogue with The Beloved.

I would tell her: you will experience a loneliness like no other. Sometimes you'll be in the presence of others and you'll feel alone because unconsciously you're grieving the loss of a previous life and struggling to adopt a new one. You'll lose friends and family. You'll even lose yourself because no one speaks of the silent identity crisis that comes with embracing Islam. An identity crisis that often surfaces many, many years down the line. When it comes, and most likely it will, hold on.

I would tell her: revisit the reasons why you became Muslim especially when many reasons present themselves to you to leave – reasons often presented at the hands of Muslims themselves.

I would tell her: everything you'll go through is a part of Allah's Plan. One day you'll set up a charity to support others because of all the trials you endured in those early years; young, alone, unsupported.

I would tell her: this is a sunnah (tradition) of life. Everything – good and bad – is with its own purpose. There is purpose in pain. Allah has a great plan for you. He has a great plan for all of us.

I would tell her: you chose Islam to save your soul. Ironically you'll forget that along the way and place others before your soul – sometimes your nearest and dearest.

I would tell her: every time you place others before your soul, life will teach you that this is never the way and actually simply the path that leads to internal suffering.

I would tell her: your soul is the most precious thing to you in this dunya (the life of this world) and just as you chose it then, you must continue to choose it now – every day, in every experience, until your last day and until your last breath.

I would tell her: live life prioritising Allah and your soul and you will get through this dunya. And if you continue to choose Allah and your soul as you did back then, then you will find Allah choosing you in small and big ways in this life – providing a sweetness of faith that even surpasses the sweetness you tasted the day you became Aliyah.

What we go through day to day, week to week, month to month and year to year can leave us feeling exhausted. Life is not easy. Add to that all we are carrying of our past and the load of all that we are nervously anticipating of the future – it can sometimes feel too much. Without pause and reflection, the days of our lives are laden with emotions of regret, sadness, lethargy and anxiety.

When our Creator designed us, He knew we could not keep going without rest. He knows that in order for us, His creation, to keep going, we need time to recuperate and re-energise. Just as He created the night for rest and sleep after a hard day, He also created periods of time in the year as much needed spiritual 'holidays' because He knows our souls cannot keep journeying towards Him without moments of pause to refuel. Today is Day 1 of the much-anticipated spiritual holiday, Ramadan. It is a spiritual prescription for all that we go through throughout the year. It has been prescribed by Allah who is better than any doctor. He knows you. He knows what you need to keep journeying towards Him and the ultimate goal – His Pleasure and the akhirah.

In the magnificent hills and mountains of Arabia, before Prophethood was granted to our beloved Messenger (ﷺ), we find a lesson for ourselves. Pause, retreat and reflection are necessary life-long prescriptions.

In the midst of so much immorality in Makkah, Muhammad (ﷺ) did not escape to a person or people. He did not escape to something which would simply numb his disturbance, confusion or pain. He escaped to solitude, to silence, to nature, to creation, contemplation and prayer. It was here that he found solace in reflection. It was here that Allah turned to him and gifted him with Divine revelation.

It is here, during moments of reflection, that you too will be gifted with lessons, growth and a closeness to your Lord.

It is vitally important for us to regularly take breaks from the normal grind of life, seclude ourselves and immerse ourselves in contemplation. This early lesson in the Prophet's life teaches us to step away from routine and make a conscious decision to pause.

We must create space in our schedules. In doing so, we silence the noise around us, which enables us to hear what Allah is telling us. We must sit with ourselves – all of ourselves: the past of ourselves, the present of ourselves and the future of ourselves – and move towards a place of truly accepting and embracing all of who we are. We must sit comfortably with solitude to experience the Company and Guidance of the Divine.

We must, because if we do not, we will simply continue being dragged along by the current of life – swept away by life's demands and responsibilities. We will continue to be susceptible to triggers from our past; emotionally reacting in a way that does not serve our present nor align with our spiritual goals. We may even find ourselves irrationally creating horror movies in our minds about our worries and concerns for the future – binding ourselves with our limiting thoughts.

In the beauty and stillness of the mountains, the Prophet thought, pondered and contemplated about life – his life, the lives of others and the meaning of life itself. This was only possible once he removed himself temporarily from the hustle and bustle of everyday life.

And so too must you retreat.

On this first day of Ramadan, I invite you to turn inwards. Focus your heart on the awakening you feel inside of you right now. It may be a quiet little flicker. It may be a loud burning flame of 'Oh my God! I need to change my life right now!' Whatever it is, it is time to make a firm resolve to regularly retreat and reflect.

During your time of reflection, your heart may need to consider the events of the last year; maybe it is what happened yesterday. Maybe it is to reflect on your childhood, which seems to unconsciously creep into your adulthood. Perhaps it is what you said or what was said to you moments before you read these words. Maybe it is to take stock of everything that has led to where you are right now in your life. Whatever needs reflection – consciously decide to do so.

Reflection is necessary. Your soul, your life depend on it.

There is no better time to take this prescription than during the days and nights of this truly blessed month. Through spiritual reflection, you can become attuned to who you really are. You will be able to see your current life for what it actually is and experience what it truly means to attain taqwa – a special spiritual closeness to Allah born from your consciousness of Him that leads you to Him, through action and worship.

Your soul deserves rest and reflection.

Let Your Heart Ponder . . .

'The contemplative believer who remembers Allah will begin to enjoy solitude and places of seclusion where voices and movements are hushed. There he will find strength of heart and will, and he will no longer be worried or depressed. Then he will begin to taste the sweetness of worship, of which he cannot have enough. In it, he will find abundance of pleasure and comfort – more than what he used to find in diversion and play, or in the satisfaction of worldly desires. When he experiences this state, many of the worldly concerns will disappear, as he is in a completely different world from the rest of humanity.'

Ibn al-Qayyim, *Madaarij As-Salikeen*

Du'a Invitation

My Lord, You said:

> In the creation of the Heavens and the Earth and the
> cycle of night and day, there are signs for smart people,
> who remember Allah standing, sitting and lying down,
> and think about the creation of the Heavens and Earth,
> prayerfully saying 'Our Lord, You haven't created this in
> vain, Glory be to You! Save us from the punishment of
> the Fire.'

Surah Al-Imran 3:190–91

Ya Rabbi, my Lord, it is time. It is time for me to slow down. It is time to pause – to breathe deeply and think deeply. Owner of my eyes, do not let my eyes see what I want them to see. Guide my eyes to see what You want them to see. Grant me the wisdom to know the difference. Help me discover if my life is being lived in such a way that I am making my relationship with You a priority. Show me what needs to be resolved or changed within me or around me to live with You as though I see You. And though I cannot see You, allow my reflections to lead me to live for You, because I certainly know You see me.

Journal

1. If I continue life without reflection, I will continue to . . .

....

....

....

2. I deserve to gift myself moments of reflection because . . .

....

....

....

3. Regular reflection can change the following:

....

....

....

4. My place(s) for reflection will be . . .

....

....

....

My reflections
on the topic of Reflection are . . .

DAY 2

Responsibility

One of the first conversations I had with my publisher about this book was online. As she walked me through the schedule from writing the first draft to publication, I had to clarify what I was hearing. Due to it being July and the plan being to publish in March, I was tasked with writing an entire manuscript from scratch within a month.

'That's really tight!' I exclaimed.

She looked at me with a knowing smile and said, 'I know, but it is possible.'

Immediately my thoughts dragged me to all the responsibilities in my life – family, work, home-educating my children, cooking, cleaning and the bare walls of my hallway, which still had not been re-wallpapered months after stripping them!

After the online meeting ended, I slumped back into my chair. I knew I had a choice. I could either succumb to my beliefs that I was too busy and it was impossible to write a book in a month, or take responsibility and say to myself, 'Aliyah – you can do this. He brought it to you. And He will get you through it. With Allah anything is possible. But in order to do this, you need to cut down on social media, cease social visits, pause netball for a few weeks, let the cleaning go and just do the absolute basics and delegate work to colleagues.'

Yet on the tenth day of my writing month, I hadn't written the ten chapters I had perfectly planned out. I had romanticised writing each day in quaint little coffee shops with Tower Bridge as my view. Sitting at my desk in the corner of my bedroom, I was feeling anxious that I was four chapters behind! The washing basket was overflowing; I was sixteenth in the queue to speak to my doctor; I had another work deadline that could not wait and in my very stressed-out state, I snapped at one of my children and, to top it all off, instead of my normal home-cooked dinner, I bunged fish fingers and chips in the oven for dinner!

I felt like the world's worst mother, which led to thoughts of: 'I'm not the right person to write this book.' I felt completely unable. I believed my thoughts and feelings were true. Feeling sorry for myself, all I could see was my sheer inability.

In that state, my thoughts led me to an image that instantly created a mental shift. I saw hands holding a book – this book. With that image came hope. The image was so vivid, the feeling was so strong and powerful, I knew I had to choose a different response.

I made a choice to take full responsibility for all of my choices – both good and bad, and to look back and take all the lessons necessary. This in turn required me to revisit and choose to take responsibility again and again.

With my vision came a realisation: whatever we are not changing is in fact a choice. And we are only truly able to see this when we consciously take time out to reflect.

Responsibility can be broken down into two words: response-ability.

Having response-ability means you are a person who has full ability to choose your response. This is fact, just as it is fact that the sun rises in the East and sets in the West. Ramadan is a month in the year when we are taught that we have full ability to go against the grain. We are able to wake up in the early hours of the morning before sunrise to eat our first meal. We are able to continue with study, work and life's demands while abstaining completely from food and drink, our energy replenished between sunset and sunrise. We are able to easily part with our money to help others. We are able to spend our nights praying in the mosque and go without sleep before we awaken to repeat it all over again for twenty-nine or thirty days!

Ramadan teaches us we are response-able.

Responsibility is not only about taking ownership of what you need to do to make something happen. Responsibility is also taking ownership of all that has happened.

Revisiting and re-examining the past to become more responsible, can feel like cleaning out old wounds. Some of those wounds may have been inflicted by people close to us or strangers, while some wounds are self-inflicted. They are painful to clean out. But in order to heal, move on and start anew, it's a necessary part of the process which cannot be skipped.

We have all experienced pain. We are all in the same boat. Some of us will sit in the boat, wallow in our circumstances and allow ourselves to drift wherever the river decides to take us. There are also those of us who accept that this is where we are, this is how we got here – this is what Allah has decreed, and we sit up straight knowing we have power, agency and choice to take the oars, place them in the water and row the boat to destinations we want to go.

I had a childhood friend who grew up in a violent home where she would witness her father beat her mother black and blue. She had two brothers close in age. One of her brothers escaped the daily abuse by turning to the wrong crowd. He became addicted to heroin – blaming the situation at home for his many stints in prison and his years spent in and out of rehab. The other brother escaped the daily abuse by turning towards sport, youth work and Allah, determined that these ugly circumstances would not define him or his life. Two brothers. Same household. One allowed the river of life to take his boat in any direction – landing him in worse waters. The other said, 'I didn't ask for this. I take responsibility for my life and this is where I want to go', and rowed his boat in that direction.

Blaming life and other people places you in a needy position where you are unable to move forward until there is an apology, a mistake rectified or a tangible change in another person. How long are you going to wait? And if the aim of Ramadan is to become truly conscious of the King of Kings, how possible is it to attain this, if your energy, thoughts and emotions are engrossed with the actions, or lack thereof, of His Creation instead of Him?

You will always be on the receiving end of what others do to you. You are not responsible for their actions. You are responsible for how you choose to respond. Your emotions are your own and owned by you. Others will trigger your emotions but they do not cause them to come into the world. You are and will always be responsible for how you respond. When you internalise this truth, you will set yourself free. And oh my, what a feeling it is to feel free.

My dear reader, whatever has come to pass – you are not a failure. There is no failure. There is no failure in how you handled what was done to you. There is no failure in how someone 'failed' you. There is no failure in your perceived shortcomings. What there is, are lessons – beautiful lessons – individually created for you by the Best Teacher because He knows what you've been through, are going through and will go through. And this is why there is no failure. This is why His Lessons for you are perfect. Because He knows you and loves you.

During this blessed month, make a choice to reposition yourself, not as a victim but as a believer who is fully responsible and able. Make a choice to stop cheating on your future and your akhirah with your past by emphatically saying, 'No! That relationship is over!'

To wake up in the morning taking full ownership for all that has happened in your life gives you a fresh start every day. You can, by His Permission, live positively, passionately, with faith, with love, acceptance and choice. To do so is freeing, liberating, fulfilling and exemplifies your belief that 'whatever He has decreed for me was best for me – and I am choosing to accept that and move forward with that'.

Your soul is too precious to hand over to another human being. It belongs to the Lord of the Worlds. The sooner you own your state of being and accept full responsibility for your state, the sooner you can focus on the most important job you have on this earth – to worship Allah and return your soul back to Him.

So, how do you do this?

Start by acknowledging that you need Allah to be your Help and Guide. Call upon your Lord who only wants you to take a step towards Him, so that He may rush to you.

Now, claim every setback you've experienced, every mistake, every wrong decision, anything you have been subjected to. How you see all of it and what you do with all of it is yours to own.

Next, realise this: Where you are right now is as a result of every choice you've made, every thought you have had, everything you have felt. Some of your choices may not have been the best but own them all. Where you are right now is a result of everything that was given to you and taken away from you by Him. All of it was absolutely best for you. Own it.

Internalise this truth in the chambers of your heart, deep in your gut and in the depths of your soul.

Now go out there and continue this journey of attaining taqwa as a believer seeking to know Allah, knowing that through becoming conscious of Him, you become conscious of how to embody response-ability in this one chance at life.

Stand tall. Shoulders back. It is time to take responsibility for who you are and where you are.

Let Your Heart Ponder . . .

'Allah never changes the condition of a nation until they change what is in themselves.'

Surah Ar-Rad 13:11

Du'a Invitation

I am Your servant. You are my Creator. You brought me into existence because I am meant to be here. Ya Allah, because I am meant to be here – I know that everything that is connected to my existence is also with purpose. I accept this. I submit to this. I embrace this. Al-Qadir, You are All Powerful and Able, I ask You to strengthen me to take responsibility for all that has passed and comes to pass in my life. Make me a believer who is at cause and lives proactively. Grant me the ability to be most responsible in regards to my journey to You.

Journal

1. What are you avoiding right now that may aid your growth? Can you turn ever so slightly towards it?

....

....

2. By doing so, what is now possible?

....

....

3. Write down all your perceived failures. Next to each one, write down what might be the Divine lesson for you.

....

....

4. By not taking responsibility, what are you choosing?

....

....

5. By taking responsibility, what are you choosing?

....

....

6. Choose a painful and difficult moment from your life. From a position of responsibility, rewrite your narrative.

....

....

My reflections
on the topic of
Responsibility are . . .

DAY 3

Love

One of my earliest childhood memories was of my mother informing me about my birth. I must have been younger than ten years old when I sat on the edge of her bed looking at her reflection in the dressing-table mirror as she recounted the story of my arrival in this world. I watched her apply her famous electric-blue mascara.

Aiming the brush at her eyelashes, she said, 'When you were born, your father missed the birth. I almost died due to kidney problems. When he arrived at the hospital, the first thing he asked me was, "What is it?" I looked over at you with so much love and told him, "It's a girl." He asked me again and I told him again, "It's a girl." He asked me, "Are you sure?" I said, "Of course, I'm sure." He then walked over to you and undid your nappy to check if you were a girl. He had wanted his first child to be a boy.'

We are all products of how much love we have or have not received. Some of us were enveloped in love from a young age. Others of us have spent and are indeed spending years trying to find the love we never had.

On this third day of Ramadan, I have something to tell you: you are loved so very much, if only you knew!

One of my favourite quotes by the thirteenth-century scholar Ibn al-Qayyim, known as the Doctor of Hearts, says,

> The heart, in its journey to Allah (ﷻ), is like that of a bird: love is its head, and fear and hope are its two

wings. When the head and two wings are sound, the
bird flies gracefully; if the head is severed, the bird dies;
if the bird loses one of its wings, it then becomes a
target for every hunter or predator.

Reading this quote, I know that without love there is death.

The absence of love in a marriage leads to the death of a
marriage. The absence of love from parent to child leads to the
emotional and psychological death of a child. The absence of
love in society leads to the death of its people.

And the absence of love in one's relationship with Allah leads
to death of faith.

So far, on this journey, you have gifted and empowered yourself with two choices that will bring about so much benefit in
your life. You have chosen to take time out to pause and reflect.
You have made the decision to take full responsibility for
everything that has happened and will happen in your life.

The next step is love. It must be love because without love
there will continue to be death on a journey that is all about
life. In fact, there will be death in two lives: this life where we
aim to live consciously with God in pursuit of the second and
last eternal life.

Let me ask you a question. What for you is the most beautiful
part of nature and Allah's creation? Maybe you're a plant lover
and marvel in the designs and colours found in the plant world.
Perhaps you love cats and get lost in their feline elegance. Perhaps it is standing in front of the ocean, the vastness taking your
breath away. Maybe it is the colours painted across the sky as
the sun wakes up and goes to sleep.

All of this is astoundingly beautiful. All of Allah's creation is
beautiful. Anything of beauty belongs to an Artist who possesses
Perfection, Beauty and Love.

I have something to tell you: you too are a part of His Beautiful Creation.

You are meant to be here, just as you are. You were created

by the same Lord who created the sparkling stars in the night sky. You were created by the same Lord who created all the beauty you see around you. He brought you into existence, in your exact form, as you are with Beauty and Love.

What does this mean? It means you matter because you are here and were created by Him. You are important, you are special and you are loved by the Most Loving, the Disposer of Affairs who manages the lives of billions of creatures every single day.

Regardless of whether you have received love or not from those who are meant to love you, you are loved by the One who truly matters. The One you came from and the One you will return to.

Internalise that. Feel it completely. I wish I could reach out to you from within these pages, and embed what you have just read deep into your heart. If there is anything you take from this book, let it be this: Allah loves you.

When we truly believe this and live life every day with this absolute truth, a huge transformation will take place – and what better month than Ramadan for this transformation? Ramadan is an invitation to transform by attaining taqwa (God-consciousness). To be conscious of Allah as a Loving Lord whose love for you is proven through His creation of you is the first step in truly getting to know Him.

One of Allah's Names is Al-Wadood, translated often as The Most Loving. The true meaning of Al-Wadood can be found in the root word, Wud, which means an intense love that is manifest. Al-Wadood is a Lord who loves so intensely that He manifests it in those whom He loves. What greater manifestation of love is there than to create something or someone that you love?

It is when we are full to the brim with Allah's Love that we are then able to love ourselves. When we are worthy in the Sight of the One who owns all that is within the East and the West, by the very fact that we exist, we will be able to acknowledge our true worth.

And when we love ourselves, we are able to love others and find opportunities to receive love and give love.

All of this is preserved beautifully in one of my favourite hadith qudsi (Allah's Words as shared by the Prophet (ﷺ)):

> My servant draws not near to Me with anything more loved by Me than the religious duties I have enjoined upon him, and My servant continues to draw near to Me with supererogatory works so that I shall love him. When I love him, I am his hearing with which he hears, his seeing with which he sees, his hand with which he strikes and his foot with which he walks. Were he to ask [something] of Me, I would surely give it to him, and were he to ask Me for refuge, I would surely grant him it. I do not hesitate about anything as much as I hesitate about [seizing] the soul of My faithful servant: he hates death and I hate hurting him.

> Bukhari

My dear reader, the very act of internalising Allah's Love for you is a deed that draws you closer to Him. To possess the correct perception of Allah is a good deed in and of itself. To place the belief that you are loved by Him in your heart, as per this hadith qudsi, in fact leads you to His Love. As Allah tells us, when He loves us, He is our hearing with which we hear others. He is our sight with which we see others. He is our hand and feet with which we move to and for others. This is profound. When we believe with certainty that Allah loves us, we are then able to hear, see and feel true love. We are able to move towards love. Because Allah has now influenced our senses with His Love.

I invite you to take a moment to reflect.

Sit with the fact, of which there is no doubt, that Allah loves you. Sit with it until you feel it within. Do not move from your place. Feel it ignite and allow it to spread, filling you with warmth within.

With that feeling and certitude that Allah loves you, it is time to take responsibility for all the ways you may have failed to love God, yourself and others. What has this meant for you? What has it led to and what have you lost? This may feel painful. I want you to know, it's okay. It really is.

This exercise is to remind you the past is there to offer us lessons. There is no failure, only beautiful lessons.

Take them as you move forward on this journey to attain taqwa.

Focus again on that feeling that Allah loves you. Intensify it. Allow it to spread everywhere – right to the very edge of your fingertips.

Infused with His Love, you can make changes in how you choose to love yourself, others and your Lord. And know this, this journey of taqwa, of worship from consciousness of Him, is the highest form of love for Allah. And with it, it transforms all other worldly love.

You are loved by the Most Loving. With that Love, choose love.

Let Your Heart Ponder . . .

'Glory be to Him whose Love for His slaves
precedes their love for Him. He praises them for
the blessings that He has already granted them.
He rewards them for what He already provided for
them. He values their imperfect traits just because
He favours them; thus, He boasts about them

for their fasting and declared that the bad smell resulting from their fasting is beloved to Him!'

Ibn al-Jawzi, *Sayd Al-Khater*

'Go after the Love of Allah and when you find it, you'll realise that you only got there because He loved you in the first place.'

Aliyah Umm Raiyaan and Farhia Yahya, Fajr Literary

Du'a Invitation

Rabbi, how can I not love You? You created me. My love for You comes from You. The more love I have for You, the more love You show me. For You have granted me the little knowledge I have of You, to love You. Everything that I enjoy in this world is a gift from You. How can I not love You? I am only able to love You by Your Will. I love You for You are my Companion when I am alone. You are my Comfort when I am sad. You are my Strength when I am weak. You push me forward when I hold back. You forgive me easily and deal with me as who I am now, not who I was. You generously reward the little good I do. You guide me when I lose my way. I and my life are between Your Fingers, yet You give me chance after chance. You reward me for something You inspired me to do. Your Doors of Mercy are open for the mistakes I chose to do. How can I not love You? You love me. And I love You. I long for the day I can meet You. Until then I take in the world You created and fall in love with a glimpse of You through Your creation, though You are Superior and more perfect than anything of Your creation I can perceive. Al-Wadood, The Most Loving, fill my heart with endless love for You. Guide me to place my worth within the realms of Your Love. Show me how to love for Your Sake.

Journal

1. I know that I am loved by Allah because . . .

....

....

....

....

2. With full certainty that Allah loves me, I am going to love Him by loving myself in the following ways . . .

....

....

....

....

3. I choose to spread love by . . .

....

....

....

....

**My reflections
on the topic of Love are . . .**

DAY 4

Gratitude

When I moved from London to the Atlas Mountains of North Africa, I lived in a small Berber village where no one else spoke English. Old women dressed in their multi-coloured dresses would sit together as they hand-washed clothes, catching up on village gossip in their Amazigh mother tongue. It took a twenty-minute drive to get to the nearest supermarket. We would climb a steep hill to collect fresh mountain drinking water, carrying litres back down again. Electricity blackouts occurred regularly and water had to be used sparingly as the government would sometimes only switch water on once a week. Large aluminium water containers remained empty – waiting to be filled for baths, toilets and kitchen use. I remember a three-week stint with no water and six people using the toilet. You can imagine the rest.

When I first moved to the mountains, I could only see problems, hardship and loneliness. Yet I lived surrounded by the sort of beauty that made me wonder, 'If this is here in this world, what must Jannah – Paradise – be like?' Focusing on what was difficult and missing filled me with sadness, frustration and resentment. I longed to return to London and found abundant examples to prove how truly difficult mountain living was.

And then, a turning point occurred. I remember the price of bananas had sky-rocketed to a ridiculous amount per kilo. As a result, one of my banana-loving sons had to go without the fruit for months. It was a matter of cost and principle. When the price finally lowered, I jumped into our car and drove round the bending roads as I descended the mountains to the nearest market place and bought a kilo of bananas. When my son returned home and found a bunch of bananas on the table, he looked at me with eyes and mouth wide open. His mouth slowly turned into a huge smile and he jumped up and down punching the air with excitement. I watched on as he gobbled up one of the bananas with pure delight. Wiping his mouth on his sleeve, he walked over to me and put his arms around my waist and said, 'Thank you, Ummi.'

As he climbed the stairs to his bedroom, I too smiled. It was in that moment that I thanked Allah for teaching my son gratitude and for making my son my teacher, who in turn taught me gratitude.

My perspective shifted and I began to see not what was missing, but what was there. I saw the beautiful mountains that surrounded our house. I saw the sea as it peeked through the parting between the two mountains. I saw the health of my children, the fact that I could provide for them when many in the village could not. With no gas pipes there to provide central heating, I thanked Allah for the electrical heaters that we would wheel over to wherever we were sitting in the bitter winter months. I thanked Allah for our beautiful home that we had worked so hard to build. I saw large blessings and small blessings and, as I thanked Allah, I began to change. I felt full. I felt blessed and I felt complete.

The realisation of how much Allah loves us and blesses us leads the heart to feel an overwhelming sense of appreciation. The path of taqwa cannot be one without gratitude.

Taqwa is to be conscious of Allah in all the ways that He is Generous, Supportive and Kind towards us in the days of our lives. Gratitude most certainly takes us to Him ('azza wa jal).

Sometimes it is only in the absence of something that we are taught gratitude. This could not be more true than in the month of Ramadan. We become grateful for the food we can no longer eat, the drink that quenched our thirst whenever we chose to, and time which is filled in these busy days and nights of worship.

We do not need to wait for absence in order to appreciate. In fact, the grateful one is one who is grateful in the presence and absence of things and people, and at times when Allah gives and withholds.

Gratitude is a choice.

Interestingly, gratitude is the translation of the Arabic word 'shukr'. Ibn al-Qayyim explains this as meaning 'the effect food has on the body of an animal'. When an animal eats, it becomes visibly heavier. Shukr then is the manifestation of Allah's blessings on a person – and the servant witnessing that.

In December 2020, Allah taught me another lesson in gratitude. Our beautiful home burnt down to the ground when lightning hit external electrical cables which struck the roof of our house, setting it alight. We lost everything. I was recording an episode for the YouTube show *Honest Tea Talk* when I heard the news. I remember whispering to myself the following remembrance of God: 'Inna lillahi wa inna ilayhi rajioun' (to Him we belong and to Him we return) – wanting to be that believer who turns to Allah with patience and gratitude right at the onset of a test.

In seconds, my mind fed me flashbacks of how hard we had worked, saving as much as we could, leaving everything behind in the UK to start a new life there. It was then that I had another realisation. Blessings are given and taken away. Gratitude is to attribute all blessings to Allah. To be thankful for when they are in your possession and to be thankful for them when they are taken away. Gratitude is also being grateful to Allah for who He is. In this instance, it was to be grateful for His timing of when He granted us our house and when He decided to take it away – believing and trusting that, for reasons unknown to us, this was surely best for our dunya and akhirah.

Gratitude does something incredible to the soul. In a research study, 300 students who were seeking mental health counselling were split into three groups. The first group were asked every week to write a letter of gratitude to someone else. The second group were asked to write about their deepest feelings about their negative experiences and the third were asked to do nothing. Those who wrote the gratitude letters reported significantly better mental health than the other two groups, four to twelve weeks after their writing exercise ended.

Allah says in the Qur'an,

And thank Allah, if you truly worship Him.

Surah Baqarah 2:172

Our purpose in life is to worship Allah. In this verse, He tells us that to truly worship Him, we must be grateful to Him. Allah tells us that our purpose, which is to worship Him, is conditional to gratitude.

On the road of taqwa, we need to cultivate a practice of gratitude. We need it for ourselves. Gratitude to Allah does not add or take away from His Perfection. The need is for us. Without it, there is no taqwa, and without taqwa, there is no real relationship with Allah. And when there is no relationship with Allah, there is a void that we try to fill with everything but it can never be filled except by coming close to Him. Gratitude then is a light on the path to our Lord.

I invite you to pause for a moment and count your blessings. Before you do, let us take the advice of the Prophet (ﷺ) who said,

Look at those below you and do not look at those above you, for it is the best way not to belittle the favours of Allah.

Bukhari and Muslim

Recall the kindness that has encompassed you since you graced the world; big and small, your inner qualities, your skills and qualifications, the people you love in life, your health, wealth, possessions, opportunities. The ways in which He has sustained you, protected you and supported you. The way Allah has covered your mistakes. The times He diverted you from something or brought you to something or someone, or led something or someone to your very door. For the times He elevated you when others put you down. For the experiences of joy, happiness, excitement, pleasure. For the tests that brought you lessons and growth. And finally, the greatest blessing of all – a robust faith.

If you were to count Allah's gifts, you would not be able to count them.

Surah Ibrahim 14:34

The more you thank Allah, the more your eyes will see the hidden and forgotten blessings in your life.

Thinking back to your past, now go a step further and thank Allah for who He has been to you and for you. Feel and show gratitude for Him being Al-Mujeeb, the One who answered your du'a; for Him being Ar-Razzaq, the One who provided you with everything you need to survive and the extra blessings you enjoy. Thank Him for being Al-Hadi, the One who guided you to Islam, to Him, to opportunities and success. Feel gratitude for Him being your Rabb who nourishes, protects and provides for you regardless of your sins and mistakes. Show immense gratitude for Him being Ar-Rahman – The Most Merciful – who gifted you this blessed month to be forgiven, to be drawn close to Him – when many people who were longing for it met the angel of death instead.

So which favours of your Lord will you deny?

Surah Rahman 55:47

Imagine a life without knowing Allah. Alhamdulillah (all praise and thanks are due to Allah) for knowing Him, loving Him and experiencing His Love.

Having thanked Allah for His Blessings and for His Being, it is now time to once again prove the utterance of your tongue with the actions of your limbs.

The Messenger of Allah (ﷺ) said,

> Verily, Allah Almighty loves to see the traces of blessings on His servant. He does not love one who wallows in misery and pessimism.
>
> Sunan Tirmidhi

Allah wants you to experience joy. He wants you to use His Blessings, to enjoy them, to feel absolutely fantastic about them. We are not here to live a miserable existence. Having thanked Allah for your blessings, now prove that gratitude by using them and enjoying them. A step further in the pursuit of God-consciousness is to discover how you can use these blessings to deepen your connection to Allah.

The more you observe the blessings from Allah, the more you will want to thank Him and the more you thank Him, the more you will realise your very expression of gratitude can never be enough for all that He indeed blesses you with.

And if you are led to gratitude, know that it is Allah who brought you there. While gratitude is a light on the path to Him, it is also a light for you – because through it, you are filled with one of the most precious of riches – to truly feel content – something no money can buy. And if that is not enough, you have a Lord who says,

> If you are grateful, I will surely increase my favours to you.
>
> Surah Ibrahim 14:7

33

Thank Allah,
He will increase you.

Let Your Heart Ponder . . .

'No one dies without Allah's Knowledge, but dies at the appointed time, as approved by Allah. Anyone who wants riches of this world, We shall give him some, and whoever wants riches of the Hereafter We shall give him all; and We will reward the thankful.'

Surah Al-Imran 3:145

'Ibn Ata said, "Contentment is the calmness of the heart in what Allah has permanently chosen for the servant as being the best possible choice, and so he is pleased with it."'

Ibn al-Qayyim, *Madaarij As-Salikeen*

Du'a Invitation

Al-Hamid, The One who is Praised, I am unable to count the blessings You have bestowed upon me. You are Abundantly Generous. You provide for me without me asking. Despite my forgetfulness to thank You, You continue to bless me in so many ways. Thank You for granting me what I need. Thank You for placing hope in my heart during tough times. Thank You for Your Love and Care. Thank You for Your Mercy which accompanies me everywhere. Thank You for running towards me when all You ask is that I take a step towards You. Thank You for my life and all that it contains. Thank You for watching over me, never leaving me. Forgive me for not thanking You enough – for all that You are, all that You do and all that You bless me with. Guide my eyes and heart to become instruments of gratitude. I praise You, for everything that I am and have is because of You. You alone are worthy of all praise. Thank You for granting me the ability to thank You.

Journal

1. I am grateful for the following big blessings . . .

....

....

2. I am grateful for the following small blessings . . .

....

....

3. I am grateful for the following things He has taken away . . .

....

....

4. I am grateful because . . .

....

....

5. Knowing the hadith, 'Whoever does not thank people has not thanked Allah', I am grateful to the following people . . . because . . .

....

....

6. Now, go thank the above people and journal how that made you feel.

....

....

**My reflections
on the topic of Gratitude are . . .**

DAY 5

Fear

Within the first two years of reverting to Islam, I found myself attending a mosque that led through fear. Jumu'ah (the Friday sermon) was always a lecture that propagated fear by focusing on everything that was haram (forbidden). Naseeha (advice) would be given harshly to women who did not dress properly, did not use correct terminology or who read books that had not been approved. While I am sure the intentions were sincerely meant to keep us on the straight path, the method adopted within that community instilled so much fear that we were made to feel as though we were daily being dipped into hellfire for anything and everything.

Needless to say, this did not sit well with me. I had embraced Islam with so much fervour and passion. I had found my purpose. But this experience triggered memories of the strictness I faced from my father when growing up. Within no time at all, my zeal and yearning to learn more and worship my Lord began to slip away. I no longer felt the sweetness that came with the Shahaadah I embraced. Islam now seemed like a burden. A terrifying one. I became afraid to do anything for fear I was incurring the wrath of God.

At this point in my life as a young Muslim revert, I found myself struggling with a difficult test. The constant reminders of needing to do the right thing, or else be destined for hellfire, weakened my faith instead of strengthening it. It was in this state that I took off my hijab, stopped praying and returned to

my old lifestyle. The reminders to be ever so fearful of the Creator, in the absence of hope, had frozen my heart. It no longer
pumped the drive to practise my faith.

Time elapsed. The circumstances that first led me to question
life and embrace Islam were still there. When I began to return to
the practice of Islam, I veered towards the other end of the spec-
trum. I returned to Islam with so much hope and a conscious
decision to possess zero fear. The result – a bird who still needed
to adjust her wings before she could fly; because in the absence
of fear, I thought I could do things my own way and forego the
very blueprint given to us by Allah, preserved in the Qur'an and
Sunnah. In so doing, I was indirectly choosing myself – my method
over Allah and the path He has carved out for the betterment of
our souls. Returning once again to the words of Ibn al-Qayyim:

> The heart, in its journey to Allah (سبحانه وتعالى), is like that of a
> bird: love is its head, and fear and hope are its two
> wings. When the head and two wings are sound, the
> bird flies gracefully; if the head is severed, the bird dies;
> if the bird loses one of its wings, it then becomes a
> target for every hunter or predator.

> *Madaarij As-Salikeen*

While love and hope are spiritual and uplifting qualities, the
fear associated with our relationship with Allah can produce
uncomfortable feelings. It can seem misplaced within the heart's
quest to know Allah, love Him and live with and for Him. Yet
without this fear, we cannot move gracefully towards Allah. An
absence of fear on this journey may even obstruct our heart's
flight to Him, 'azza wa jal.

Through experience and much reading of those who have
delved deep into the spiritual journey of the heart towards
Allah, I believe the needed readjustment of the wing of fear is
found in:

1. Having a correct, healthy understanding of fear of Allah.

2. Ensuring you fear Him as much as you have hope in Him – constantly pausing to see if that balance is present in your heart, and most importantly in your actions.

Khawf (fear), in its verb form, means to fear Allah or to have fear of Him. Revisiting the loving act Allah ('azza wa jal) took in creating you, a question arises. How can we align fear of Allah with this concept of a Lord who loves us so much that He willed our existence? I believe the answer lies in the adjustment of the meaning we have associated with fear and not fear itself.

You love Allah. You know He loves you. You know your purpose is to return to Him, having earned as much of His Pleasure in this life as possible. Where and how does fear align with this?

The more you love Allah and the more you internalise His Love for you, the more you revere Him and respect Him. You become a servant who has so much love and adoration for Him that you never want Him to be disappointed with you. Even though you know your disappointing Him is met with His Abundant Mercy, which always outweighs His Wrath, you hold Him in such high regard – more than anyone or anything else in your life – that your heart bursts with so much reverence. When the lover of Allah is completely submerged in such love, a fear is experienced to be in any other state than this. There is a fear of losing His Love. There is a fear of losing the love you have in your heart for Him. There is a fear that the ways in which you show Him your love are not enough or will not be accepted.

The great scholar Imam Sufyan al-Thawri said:

I fear that my faith will be taken away at the point of death.

Aisha, the wife of the Prophet (may Allah be pleased with her), narrates:

> I said, O Messenger of Allah, does the verse 'And they who give what they give while their hearts are fearful' refer to he who commits fornication, drinks alcohol, and steals?' He said, 'No, O daughter of the Truth-lover (Abu-Bakr), but to a man who fasts, prays and gives charity, and fears that it may not be accepted from him.'
>
> Sunan Tirmidhi

Here we can see that the journey of the lover of Allah is one of striving to love and be loved by The Most High, accompanied with fear because of the extent of how precious the believer knows that love, that relationship, that end goal is. Fear, then, is the fleeing of the heart from all that will disrupt its relationship with the Beloved.

And yet, the most exquisite part of all of this is knowing you will in fact never lose His Love and that the fear of losing it causes Him to love you. Subhana'Allah (how free of any imperfection is Allah).

This is the balance found in the two wings. It is balanced by having hope that He will continue to stoke the burning flame of love within your heart. It is balanced by the fact that He is a Lord who rewards you for your intention even if you can't bring yourself to action, even if your action is flawed.

The Messenger of Allah (ﷺ) revealed that Allah, The Glorious, said:

> Verily, Allah has ordered that the good and the bad deeds be written down. Then He explained it clearly how (to write): He who intends to do a good deed but he does not do it, then Allah records it for him as a full good deed, but if he carries out his intention, then Allah

the Exalted writes it down for him as from ten to seven hundred folds, and even more. But if he intends to do an evil act and has not done it, then Allah writes it down for him as a full good deed, but if he intends it and has done it, Allah writes it down as one bad deed.

Bukhari and Muslim

By adopting a healthy understanding of fear and ensuring it is balanced with hope, we can move forward in our pursuit to make the most of this blessed month of Ramadan. We are conscious of Allah in our hope and our fear of Him. We present ourselves to His Mercy during this month, hoping for His Forgiveness, and fear doing anything that will prevent us from it.

It is then that we can truly fly to Him (ﷻ). This is beautifully portrayed in the verse from the Qur'an which says,

Indeed, those who, out of awe for their Lord, are fearful, and those who believe in their Lord's signs, and those who associate none with their Lord, and those who bring whatever they bring while their hearts tremble, knowing that to their Lord they are returning – those are the ones who hasten towards good works, and it is they who will reach it first.

Surah Al-Mu'minun 23:57–61

My dear readers, fear is a beautiful means towards the ultimate goal.

At all costs, protect your loving relationship with Him.

Let Your Heart Ponder . . .

'When true fear of Allah is realised in your heart, all good things will come to you.'

Ibn al-Jawzi, *Aqwal Ibn al-Jawzi*

'How can you deny Allah when you were dead and He brought you to life; then He will cause you to die and give you life once more, and to Him you shall be returned.'

Surah Baqarah 2:28

Du'a Invitation

Ar-Ra'uf, You are the Most Kind and I am in need of Your Kindness. I feel guilty. Guilty for not having done enough good deeds. Guilty for pursuing that which is contrary to the path I seek towards You. Though I feel this, ya Rabbi, I know that this feeling of guilt is a gift from You – that I am more conscious of You. To You, I am most grateful. You love for Your servants to turn towards You. I am turning towards You wanting to protect my relationship with You. I cannot do this without Your Help and Guidance. Place reverence in my soul for You. Increase my fear of losing my way on this journey towards You. I yearn for You to be more beloved to me than anything else. Help me protect that every day by flying to You with a balance of hope and fear.

Journal

1. What fears do I have that are negatively impacting my relationship with Allah?

....

2. What can I choose to do about those fears?

....

3. Am I veering more towards fear or hope?

....

4. What practical steps can I take to create balance?

....

5. Write out five hopes you have of Allah. To create balance, next to each one write out the healthy, beautiful 'fear' you can associate to it.

....

6. Write out five fears you have of Allah. Next to each one, write out how you can balance them with hope.

....

**My reflections
on the topic of Fear are . . .**

DAY 6

Repentance

There is a famous story told by a sheikh:

In one of the alleys a door opened and a young boy came out, crying and begging; behind him his mother was kicking him out, until she shut the door after him. The young boy hardly walked a short distance before he stopped and wondered where to go. Not finding any other way but the house from which he was thrown out, with no one to give him refuge other than his mother, he returned to her door with a broken, pained heart. Finding the door closed, he laid down by the door, resting his cheek on the doorstep, and slept. After a while, his mother came out and upon seeing him in that state, she could not hold herself back, and fell on him, holding, hugging and kissing him, crying and saying: 'My son, where will you go away from me? Who will protect you but me? Did I not warn you: do not oppose me, do not make me do through your disobedience what is opposite to what I am inclined by nature to have of mercy and compassion for you, and wishing nothing but good for you.' Then she took him and brought him in.

Ibn al-Qayyim, *Madaarj As-Salikeen*

There is a simple truth: everything we do and do not do is for the next life. In this life we will make mistakes and sin. We are all sinners, sinning differently. From sheikh to layman, rich to poor, famous to non-famous – we are all sinners.

This life then is to put forth and to withhold in ways that will earn His Pleasure – accompanied by repentance of any mistakes and sin we make along the way. Ramadan is an opportunity to be completely forgiven – as though we are as clean as the day we were born. I wish I could write an entire book on this topic alone, for it encompasses our very purpose. For the past five days, we have been looking at our past – healing, learning and taking responsibility. Yesterday we identified the need to fear losing our way with Allah. Today, I present you with a beautiful gate to step through, one that translates that fear into action. It is always open and if you step inside, it will lead you to a garden of spiritual delight.

How Allah inclines towards us with His Mercy – if only we knew! When we sin, we are temporarily separated from His Mercy. When we repent and turn back to Him, we return to that which we are entitled to, His Love and Mercy, both of which are our rights upon Him.

What better month to truly understand how beautiful the station of repentance is than this month, which the Messenger of Allah (ﷺ) described as a time where,

> Whoever fasts it with faith and expecting reward will be rid of sins like the day he was born from his mother.

> Musnad Aḥmad

And though sins are the very antithesis of journeying towards taqwa, we are told,

> If you did not commit sins, Allah would remove you and replace you with people who sin and seek forgiveness so He will forgive them.

> Muslim

I always wondered why Allah would replace us with a people who sin for those who do not.

Allah ('azza wa jal) knows your imperfection and weakness. He, who is The Perfect One, is not expecting perfection from you. He simply wants sincere effort. And in the absence of effort, where there might be mistakes and sins that you regret, He turns to you with His Forgiveness and Mercy. Such that,

> The crying of the sinners is more beloved to Allah than the glorification of Allah of the arrogant.
>
> Ibn al-Qayyim, *Madaarij As-Saalikeen*

For it is the sinner who is humbled and yearns for Allah's Forgiveness who truly embodies ubudiyyah – true servitude.

When we turn away from our purpose and sin against the One who just wants us to do our best, Allah calls us by an endearing name – 'Ibaadi (My slaves):

> Say: 'O 'Ibaadi (My slaves) who have transgressed against themselves (by committing evil deeds and sins)! Despair not of the Mercy of Allah, verily, Allah forgives all sins. Truly, He is Oft-Forgiving, Most Merciful.
>
> Surah Al-Zumar 39:53

This fills the aching heart with comfort – that despite our failings, we are told we are still His subjects; still His. We are still close to Him. He does not call us 'O sinner'. He calls upon us as 'My slaves, My servants', stating that we still belong to Him. He has not left us and we simply need to return to Him. He tells us He is full of abundant Mercy, ready to forgive.

And for those who commit major sins, Allah goes a step further and calls upon us as 'Ibadur Rahman' in Surah Furqan, verse 63. Please go read this love letter from your Lord, Most High. In response to the worst acts we could ever commit and the worst states in which we could ever find ourselves, He calls us 'The servants of the Most Merciful' – displaying closeness to us by attaching our name to His Most Beautiful Name.

All of this is a reminder: it is never too late to turn back to your Lord. Remember that your Lord's Doors of Forgiveness and Mercy are always open because He wants you, His believing servant who has sinned, to know that He is there – ready to forgive you. All you need to do is step inside.

Ramadan is a month where we turn to Allah with our mountains of sins. If you are looking at yourself in disgust for what you have done and feel as though you are drowning in despair, I need to tell you to stop.

Just stop.

Your Lord wants you to have complete hope in Him and His Mercy.

One of the biggest disservices you can do to yourself and to your Lord is to despair of His Mercy. Despair is drowning. You can't breathe. But you have the option to move your limbs and push yourself to the surface. You must change your perception – your mistakes and sins are not heavy weights pulling you down further into the water. Your Lord is not pushing you down. He wants you to rise through repentance. And when you do rise, know it was only possible with His Permission as He reaches out to you with Love and Mercy.

When you choose to give in to despair, you are choosing to turn away from that which He is enabling you to do – survive, make amends, choose differently and live to tell the tale.

To have hope is faith. To despair is to turn away from faith – in Him and all that He can do and enable you to do. He says, 'Be.' And it is. Say, 'I trust. I have hope in You, my Lord.' And it will be.

And who despairs of His Lord's Mercy except for those astray?

Surah Al-Hijr 15:56

Sometimes you are so busy drowning that you fail to realise you may have already been forgiven by Him long ago because of the sincere regret that filled your heart. The only thing that is holding you back is your despair – which should not exist because you have a Lord who calls you 'O My Servant of the Most Merciful' at your lowest darkest moment. The Messenger of Allah (ﷺ) said,

> 'Allah laughs for the despair of His servant, as He will soon relieve him.' His companion asked, 'O Messenger of Allah, does the Lord laugh?' The Prophet said, 'Yes.' His companion replied, 'We will never be deprived of goodness by a Lord who laughs!'

Sunan Ibn Majah

Now, dry those tears if they are tears of despair. And cry for one reason and one reason alone: that you have a beautiful Lord who laughs, knowing forgiveness and relief is on the way. You have a Lord who forgives the greatest of sinners who has committed the greatest of sins and turns them into good deeds. He is Ar-Rahman, The Most Merciful and you are Iba-dur Rahman – the servant of the Most Merciful. Always remember that.

Repentance must accompany you on every part of this journey towards the akhirah. It must because you are living in this dunya with the Eye of your Beloved upon you. With an acknowledgment that you will sin, that there is no need to despair and that you have a Lord who loves the one who repents, I invite you to initiate a relationship with repentance that you will nurture for the rest of your life.

As you look back at your past, feel regret for all that you did which was not loved by your Beloved. This is a time when it is a beautiful state to have your heart feel like it has been ripped to pieces. As Ibn al-Qayyim wrote:

If one's heart is not torn into pieces in this world, due to regret and fear over what it has lost, it is torn in the hereafter when the truths are revealed and the reward of the obedient and the punishment of the disobedient are distributed. Thus, a broken heart is inescapable either in this world or in the eternal life.

Madaarij As-Salikeen

Realise that an aching regretful heart is a heart that is very much still pumping with imaan (faith). With regret, allow yourself to be thrown in front of your Lord – humble and needy. This state is so very much loved by Allah and is the reason why He would replace you with a person who sins and embodies servitude in such a way. This internal sensor of regret in the heart is beautiful, for if you have sinned and felt nothing, it means your heart is dead. As Ibn al-Qayyim says,

A wound does not cause pain to a corpse.

Madaarij As-Salikeen

So, even if all you feel is a second of regret or a slight uncomfortable twitch – know that your heart is still alive with faith, journeying to its Lord.

With a heart engulfed in regret – a heart which leads the limbs of a person – the most natural step you will feel compelled to take is to do all that you can to stop the sin.

Let us be honest. Some sins are ever so sweet – providing us with joy in the short term. But that's just it. It is only ever for the short term and we are living and breathing for the long term. A quick walk around a cemetery glancing at the ages of the deceased, carved permanently into marble, is a good reminder that our long term can start sooner than we think.

Some sins are easier to stop than others. You are human and

Allah knows that. He is Compassionate and Understanding. The first step is asking Allah to make it easy for you to stop your sin. Tell Him you are finding it tough. Tell Him it is just too irresistible. Be honest with yourself and come to Him vulnerably.

After asking Him for help, realise that anything to which you are attached, and which you know you must give up, needs to be replaced with something else immediately in order to afford you the distractions and strength to eventually resist it.

With a regretful heart and the cessation of that which is disliked by the Lord of the Heavens, it is time to turn to Allah with humility and say, 'O my Lord, I am truly sorry.'

The Prophet (ﷺ) said:

> Whoever says it during the day with firm faith in it and dies on the same day before the evening, he would be from the people of Paradise; and whoever recites it at night with firm faith in it and dies before the morning, he will be from the people of Paradise:

> > Oh Allah, You are my Lord. None has the right to be worshipped but You. You created me and I am Your slave, and I am faithful to my covenant and my promise to You as much as I can. I seek refuge with You from all the evil I have done. I acknowledge before You all the blessings You have bestowed upon me, and I confess to You all my sins. So I entreat You to forgive my sins, for nobody can forgive sins except You.

> > Bukhari

With regret, cessation of sin with His Help and sincere apology, prove to your Lord with actions that confirm your words.

This is tawbah (the return to Allah through repentance). This is the essence of Ramadan – to have a month in which to pause and reflect with remorse, to provide a training ground in which to stop what we normally do and to say sorry in the nights of Ramadan, proving to Allah we truly are repentant through our sacrifice, sadaqa (charity) and prayer.

We are imperfect beings traversing an imperfect journey, and so repentance must accompany us everywhere, holding ourselves to account, regretting, ceasing sins and apologising by our speech and actions, and aiming to do better next time.

Allah loves this! He loves when we repent because:

> Allah surely is more merciful to His servants than a
> mother is to her child.
>
> Bukhari and Muslim

His Mercy is such that He only sees us the way we are today. And in the past, He saw us as we were in the past. This is the way Allah deals with His servants.

Advice I was given years ago by Imam Sulayman Van Ael is so apt to share today:

> If today you worship Him – then at that very
> instance – He looks at you as being a worshipper. When
> you read Qur'an, He looks at you as someone who
> reads Qur'an. So He doesn't look at one particular thing
> in your life and judge you by it, rather that was a
> fragment within life and at that moment you would be
> judged accordingly. A person sins by lying but at the
> same time this person can be someone who prays at
> night and sincerely loves Allah. The moment he lies, he
> is a liar but the other moments he can be a worshipper
> and this does not turn someone into a hypocrite – but
> into a human being with flaws and shortcomings and
> mistakes. Expecting ourselves to be perfect is like

something that Imam Ghazali said – that it sprouts from one's high thoughts of oneself and sometimes we fall very low to then jump very high, and in so doing, we understand who we can be without Allah's Help and who we are with His Help. Allah will judge you in harmony with what you do now. If you were a sinner yesterday and turned to Him in repentance today, then you are beloved to Him. For today, you are a humble servant begging Him for forgiveness. And He loves tawbah.

The Messenger of Allah (ﷺ) said,

> Verily, Allah is more pleased with the repentance of His slave than a person who has his camel in a waterless desert carrying his provision of food and drink and it [the camel] is lost. He, having lost all hopes (to get that back), lies down in shade and is disappointed about his camel; when all of a sudden he finds that camel standing before him. He takes hold of its reins and then out of boundless joy blurts out: 'O Allah, You are my slave and I am Your Rabb.' He commits this mistake out of extreme joy.

Muslim

Repentance is loved by Allah, so much so that He tested the most honoured of creation with it. Allah is more pleased with repentance than any other good deed – highlighted in the hadith above. Through repentance, you become dear to Allah through your display of humility, neediness and praise of Him, as a sinner who turns to Allah with humility and broken-heartedness – the heart and soul of worship that leads you to Him.

Know, my dear reader, there is another thing to remember about repentance. Your repentance is enveloped by Allah's Forgiveness before and afterwards. Allah turns to you by way of granting you permission to repent, inspiring your heart to regret and pushing you towards the door of tawbah. Allah's turning towards you preceded your repentance, becoming the cause of your repentance, which shows that you cannot repent until He turns to you as The Most Forgiving. And oh my, do we have a Lord who turns to us. No greater example of this exists than the du'a we make in the last ten nights of Ramadan, where our beloved Messenger (ﷺ) advised us to say,

> O Allah, You are pardoning. You love to pardon, so pardon me.
>
> Sunan Tirmidhi

Allah turns to us after repentance with acceptance and reward. In Ramadan, this extends beyond acceptance. It is complete pardoning, from the word 'afuuw', which means to completely erase as though it did not exist. This is tawbah and the unimaginable mercy of Allah.

> If the believer knew what was with Allah of punishment, no one would hope for Paradise. If the disbeliever knew what was with Allah of mercy, no one would despair of attaining Paradise.
>
> Sunan Tirmidhi

I have one last thing to say and I want you to read this short statement carefully: if this is the relationship of repentance between servant and Lord, what then of the need to also forgive yourself?

Turn to your Lord who so very much loves the one who turns back to Him.

Let Your Heart Ponder . . .

'A person may commit a sin, which may lead him to Paradise, and one may act obediently but that may take him to hellfire.' People asked them how that could be. They said, "If one commits a sin, but then regrets it, unable to forget it and rest in peace, he laments standing, walking and lying down; he thus courts true humility, repenting and begging for forgiveness, and this leads him to Paradise. On the other hand, one who does a good deed may become filled with it; walking, sitting, lying down he remembers it and feels elated, proud and self-satisfied, until these lead him to destruction."'

Ibn al-Qayyim, *Madaarij As-Salikeen*

Du'a Invitation

Al-Ghaffar, The All-Forgiving, my heart breaks before You. I present myself humbly before You. Nothing can save me except You. I have no choice and no escape except to You. Your acceptance and happiness with me is precious to me. You know me more than I know myself. I love You and I ardently need You. I am weak. You are the One who pardons. I need Your Mercy. Have mercy upon me. I am one of many of Your servants, but You are my only Rabb. I come to You poor and needy like one whose nose has been rubbed into dirt, my eyes full of tears, my heart prostrating – humbled, forgive me.

Journal

1. Write down your own personal pledge between you and Allah to make repentance a regular priority in your life.

....

....

2. I can improve my relationship with tawbah by changing the following . . .

....

....

3. Take yourself to somewhere quiet and alone. Let your heart feel regret for all the major, minor, public and private sins you have committed; the things you can remember and the things you cannot. Write down the sins you can stop today. Spend time talking to Allah and apologising.

....

....

4. Next to each sin you can stop today, write down one thing you can replace it with and one action that will prove to Allah that your repentance is sincere.

....

....

**My reflections
on the topic of Repentance are . . .**

DAY 7

Forgiving Others

I have a close friend whose major tests in life are all related to her family. Out of all of my friends, I feel her attachment to her children is so overwhelmingly strong that Allah repeatedly brings her back to the prayer mat desperate and yearning for Him, as it is these tests with her children that draw her to Him. Others may be tested with financial or health concerns. I find my own most challenging tests have been connected to people hurting me. I have often thought why this is my reoccurring test – I believe it is intrinsically linked to the early pain of my childhood and teenage years. That pain was so raw that I have been repeatedly tested in adulthood with rejection, betrayal and disingenuous company. It is these tests that have caused me to break, cry out to Allah like never before and raise my hands towards the Heavens, begging Him to release me from the agony. It is these tests that bring me to the footsteps of a gate of Paradise in this life – the sweetness of faith, found in turning to Him desperately.

I know how agonising it is to be hurt by others. I know how very hard it is to forgive. Through my experience, I also know how necessary it is to forgive – not for the other party, but for myself. The journey of forgiving others is not a simple mathematical equation – do this and it will equate to this. It is a journey with lots of bumps, twists and turns.

Day six, we entered the gate of tawbah whereupon we found the Mercy and Forgiveness of Allah. Today, I invite you to consider this: if The Most Merciful who created the galaxies in the universe rushes to forgive you, then what is stopping you from forgiving others? I invite you to become aware of how a lack of forgiveness harms your own soul, and how forgiving others frees your soul and is a means to great reward.

Your soul is the most precious thing you own. You are carrying a lot. You are carrying enough. You were not created to carry more than you can bear.

Make this journey, piling up as many good deeds as you can, but let go of anything that you are not required to carry. One of the most precious gifts you can give to yourself is to let go of that which is hurting and harming your soul – this precious entity that will pass onto the next world. One of the most painful things we carry is the pain caused by others which leads to a secondary pain caused by ourselves as we struggle to forgive – which interferes with our journey to the eternal life.

Ramadan is the month of Allah's Mercy. As we engage in worship, hoping to be forgiven by Allah, I invite you to put your ego aside, picture yourself in your grave hearing the last footsteps walk away and absorb this chapter with every chamber of your heart.

Shaykh Ibn Baz said,

> If you train yourself to pardon people, your soul will relax, your heart will be tranquil and your rank will become great with Allah and His slaves.
>
> *Hadeeth al-Masaa'*

I love this quote because it describes the process of forgiving others perfectly. It is a form of training. We arrive maybe having an idea of what it will entail. But through training, we really learn, we pick up tools and skills. Through practice we improve. We make mistakes along the way and we learn from them – doing better next time. All with the hope of achieving a qualification.

My dear reader, that qualification is none other than your position and rank in the akhirah.

There are two types of raw pain in this world: the pain that is caused by others and the pain we endure by not forgiving. When anger, resentment and vengeance settle in our hearts this eats away at us and we end up punishing ourselves for someone else's mistakes. It is a punishment that eats away at us more than the actual action of the person who hurt us. It permeates our waking hours, our sleep, affects our relationships and worship. The actions of another human being contaminate our lives to the point that we become unrecognisable even to our self. We remain like this, sometimes for years, because we are waiting and desperately hoping for someone else to change, say sorry and truly mean it!

But here is the thing – the ability to move forward from the hurt someone else has caused you will never be forthcoming from the very hands that caused you pain. Moving forward is a choice you can take. Moving forward is a choice you must make.

If it takes forty-three muscles to frown and seventeen muscles to smile, imagine how much energy you are giving to anger, hurt and vengeance over forgiveness and peace.

Now, I need to clarify something here. Some people do some seriously horrible things. I'm with you – it feels as though they do not deserve to be forgiven. The injustice screams at you every day. However, forgiveness is not about them. It is about you. It is about you because your entire existence is either working for you or against you on this journey to the akhirah. Part of the journey of taqwa is to become better, do better and make choices that Allah will be most pleased with. It is a journey where we aspire to become muttaqeen (believers who are ever conscious of God).

Allah says,

But whoever has endured patiently and has forgiven,
this is certainly a sign of real resolve.

Surah Ash-Shura 42:43

The Messenger of Allah (ﷺ) said,

> Charity does not decrease wealth. No one forgives
> but Allah increases him in honour, and no one
> humbles himself before Allah but Allah raises him
> in status.

Muslim

And,

> There is no man who suffers an injury to his body, then
> he forgives [the one who caused it] as an act of charity,
> but Allah will absolve his sins commensurate with the
> extent of his charity.

Musnad Aḥmad

With this aspiration, if you have faced injustice, you need to separate what was done to you from who you are. Sometimes we confuse the two. What someone else did and the pain it caused you is not who you are or need to be. You are you – yes, most likely a different you after the event. There needs to be a clear mental compartmentalisation.

Dealing with it in this way allows you to live without carrying the pain. You can put it down when you need to. When something reminds you of the pain and triggers you, you can feel through all of it. And then, because it is separate from your being – put it away again.

You cannot change the past and what was done to you, but you can change your response. This does not mean you accept or forget what they did. It means you direct your attention to the reward promised by the Prophet (ﷺ):

The merciful will be shown mercy by the Most Merciful.
Be merciful to those on the earth and the One in the
heavens will have mercy upon you.

Sunan Tirmidhi

I remember a quote my daughter shared with me. Referring to parents, it said, 'This is their first time too.' Meaning that it is the first time our parents are doing this thing called life, just as we are. When I think about people who have wronged me, I cannot help but see them in this light. It's their first time at this dunya too.

I once forgave someone. And when I did, I let go. I set myself free. I felt liberated from my own shackles of hurt and resentment because I did not feel any need for acknowledgement or action from the person that hurt me. The process had nothing to do with them. It was for me. Because, in the words of the author Lewis B. Smedes, 'To forgive is to set a prisoner free and discover that prisoner is you.' I love this quote. To forgive is a verb, it means you need to do something. Not someone else, only you. It places you back in the driving seat.

Following forgiveness, perhaps a healthy distance is needed from the person that hurt you. When the Prophet (ﷺ) lost his uncle Hamza whose body was mutilated by Hind, who cut out his liver, chewed it and spat it out, he was stricken with grief. It was reported that,

We have never seen the Messenger of Allah weeping so much as he was for Hamza bin 'Abdul Muttalib.

Ibn Masud

Despite this, he (ﷺ) forgave Hind, but asked her to never come near him again as her reminder was too much for him to bear. In this we find that forgiveness can be accompanied by healthy boundaries.

Sometimes only giving people who hurt you their basic rights is what will enable you to prioritise your soul. And that's okay. Your soul, which can return to Allah at any given second, is too precious to be chained by the actions of others. With this realisation, a painful experience is turned into the pursuit of making this a stepping stone towards your Lord.

In this beautiful month of mercy, I leave with you a reflection: people are like leaves of a tree. They come and they go. We live with people as though they are leaves of an evergreen tree – always vibrantly green, permanent. There are very few people in our lives that are evergreen. Most are not and follow the simple natural cycle of a leaf. At one point, they are full of life, a deep luscious green; providing us with a source of energy. Then they begin to change – they lose their vibrancy and become almost unrecognisable. A dry, crispy yellow develops and they are no longer able to provide you with what you need. Sometimes they provide you with the very opposite. They have run their term and fulfilled their purpose for you and your life. It is hard when people change. It is hard when people hurt us. It is hard when they leave or you have to leave them. It is painful. We are left feeling alone and bare.

And yet, it is important to remind ourselves of the One who created the tree and its leaves. He will take people away from your life sometimes through pain caused by their own hands, because it is a must. It is essential for the old to leave so that the new can emerge. It is a cycle of life. What is no longer good has to leave and be replaced. What is no longer good for you has to be taken away.

Your Lord Most High is One who has created balance and order in everything – and that includes your life. Whenever someone hurts you and leaves, He will always replace that person with something or someone different; something or someone better; something or someone that is in alignment with what He knows you and your future need.

I invite you to embrace the cycle of life and the changes that come with it. Trust that people in our lives may have a course that has to come to an end. They were for then. Let us now look forward to the ones that are for now.

I firmly believe Allah sends people and what they do to us our way because either we need them to change our life, or we are the ones that will change theirs. And sometimes through this painful and yet beautiful paradox, both lives, in this life and the next, are changed by the other.

Let go. Forgive.
Your soul deserves it.

Let Your Heart Ponder . . .

'Anas ibn Malik reported: We were sitting with the Messenger of Allah, and he said, "Coming upon you now is a man from the people of Paradise." A man from the Ansar came whose beard was dishevelled by the water of ablution and he was carrying both of his shoes with his left hand. The next day the Prophet repeated the same words, and the man came in the same condition. The third day the Prophet repeated the same again, and the man came in the same condition. When the Prophet stood up to leave, Abdullah ibn . Amr followed the man and he said, "I am in a dispute with my father and I have sworn not to enter my home for three days. May I stay with you?" The man said yes.

Abdullah stayed three nights with the man but he never saw him praying at night. Whenever he went to bed, he would remember Allah and rest until he woke up for morning prayer. Abdullah said that he never heard anything but good words from his mouth. When three nights had passed and he did not see anything special about his actions, Abdullah asked him, "O servant of Allah, I have not been in dispute with my father nor have I cut relations with him. I heard the Prophet say three times that a man from the people of Paradise was coming to us and then you came. I thought I should stay with you to see what you are doing that I should follow, but I did not see you do anything special. Why did the Prophet speak highly of you?" The man said, "I am as you have seen." When Abdullah was about to leave, the man said, "I am as you have seen, except that I do not find dishonesty in my soul towards the Muslims and I do not envy anyone because of the good that Allah has given them." Abdullah said, "This is what you have achieved and it is something we have not accomplished."'

Musnad Aḥmad

Du'a Invitation

The All-Knowing, The All-Seeing, The All-Hearing – I am Your servant. You are Al-Hakam, The Judge. I am bringing the injustice, hurt and pain to Your Court. I have been oppressed. You have promised me You hear the oppressed. Hear me today. I hand over the way I have been oppressed to You. You are Perfect in Your Justice. I trust You, Al-Adl – The Most Just. I choose to no longer carry this. I hand over my case to You. In doing so, I let go and trust that You will manage what has occurred in the best of ways and at the perfect time. I ask You to free me from the shackles of what they did and to cleanse my heart of any feeling that is taking me away from my journey to You. I hand it all over to You. I am Your servant and You are my Lord. They are Your servants and You are their Lord. I choose to move forward from this with You and to You. I ask You to rectify their affairs and to forgive them. Just as my Prophet said, 'Forgive them, for they do not know.'

Journal

1. Choosing to hold onto anger, resentment and pain has created the following disruption in myself, my relationships and in my faith . . .

....

....

....

....

2. I choose to prioritise my soul and change that by . . .

....

....

....

....

3. I look forward to this changing my life in the following ways . . .

....

....

....

....

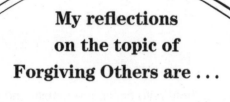

**My reflections
on the topic of
Forgiving Others are . . .**

....

....

....

....

....

....

....

....

....

....

....

....

DAY 8

Qadr

On my twenty-first Shahaadah anniversary, I wrote the following:

As I contemplate beginnings and ends – health and illness, company and solitude, life and death – I look back at my last twenty-one years as a believing soul . . . Oh, how I would have done so many things differently. I'm sure we're all thinking the same for one reason or another: how we wish we could turn back the hands of time and have chosen and decided differently.

But all of it was meant to be. All of it was written long before we came into existence. We were meant to make the decisions we made; married the people we married; fallen ill at the time we did; lost when we did; gained when we did; and arrived at certain realisations when we did.

I've been through a rough ride this last year and it's far from over. So many tests have hit me – one after the other without a gap of relief in between. Life sometimes takes a turn like that. I've complained. I've questioned. I've felt down. Some days I haven't dealt with my tests as I would have hoped.

But then I remind myself, 'Aliyah, you're human.' And then I inhale and exhale slowly. I silence my thoughts and immerse myself in the beauty of His Creation, thus reminding myself of Him.

Then, I remember.

I remember everything happened at the perfect time; in the most perfect way; with the perfect people; in the most perfect of circumstances – even if I perceive some or all of it to be 'bad'.

I remind myself again that I'm human and sometimes I'll lose sight of this. Sometimes I'll forget my belief in decree – the good of it and the bad of it – the acceptance of it and the belief it is all good because it comes from the One who possesses all that is good. And that's okay.

Upon remembering, I take my belief in qadr (Divine Decree) deep into my heart: I was where I was meant to be then. And right now I'm right where I'm meant to be now – even if that is right in the midst of a storm. And Allah knows where I'll be in the future is exactly where I'm meant to be.

Ramadan is one of the most blessed months in the year. And of its nights, Laylatul Qadr (the Night of Decree) is the most blessed. The famous Islamic scholar Hasan al-Basri said,

> . . . all the affairs of lifespan, deeds, creation, and provision are decreed on Laylatul Qadr in the month of Ramadan and will come to pass in the coming year.

Al-Bayhaqi, Kitab Fada'il al-Awqat

The knowledge of when Laylatul Qadr is was withheld from us, and from this comes a striving from billions of Muslims around the world to witness it, worship extensively in it and ask of Allah – hoping for His Response and reward.

We are still in the first third of Ramadan and have twelve days until we begin to seek out Laylatul Qadr. With this in mind, let us look back at our past to discover the treasures that lie in this pillar of faith – to believe in what has been predestined, in what has been written.

When I think about qadr, I experience a warm sensation inside. Over the years it has provided me with great comfort with my tests with people. One of the things I love most about this beautiful deen (way of life) that Allah guided me to is the belief that everything has been written. I am in love with Al-Wakil – The Best Disposer of Affairs. Much of my writing on social media is connected to qadr. And I hope that what I write today touches your heart and develops a trust deep within for the One who 'has your back' completely.

As I too look back at my past, I see a beautiful pattern emerge. You yearn for what you want, you ask for what you want; Allah, in His Infinite Wisdom, gives you what you need. All we are required to do is believe, trust and submit to His Knowledge and Will.

When amazing things emerge in our life – a goal-orientated opportunity, an answered du'a, a job, a spouse – it is easy to believe in qadr. It is easy to attribute these wonderful things to Allah ('azza wa jal) and to believe He is the Best Planner of our affairs.

On the other hand, when we are hit with what we do not want – sometimes the very things we have been begging Allah to never test us with – our belief in qadr can feel shaky and we are put to the test. But subhana'Allah, it is these very challenging circumstances that develop our belief in qadr and our full trust and reliance upon Allah, Al Wakil, in a way nothing else does.

I remember reading a verse from Surah Yunus. Isn't it amazing how you can read a verse that you have read so many times before, but the day you need it, it just reads and hits you differently? The verse I read was,

. . . Allah's alone is the knowledge of what is beyond the reach of human perception.

Surah Yunus 10:20

It touched me deeply because we live our lives expecting, scheduling, anticipating, planning. Part of being a Muslim – one who submits to the Owner of the Universe – is to submit to His Plan by wholeheartedly accepting that His Plan is always for the best. This can only come from a heart that deeply internalises and lives with the absolute fact that He Sees and Knows that which we never can. His Knowledge encompasses the future before our future becomes our reality. He already knows our tomorrow when we have not even finished our today.

We have zero knowledge of what will happen in the next second, let alone tomorrow. When we were foetuses in the wombs of our mothers, His Knowledge encompassed our date of birth, our name, our closest friend, the places we would call home, the names of our teachers and tutors, whether we would marry and who that would be, whether we would have children – their gender and number, the illnesses we would be tested with, the people that would bring us joy and pain, when we would leave this world and how we would leave it.

As you read these words, He knows what will happen to you in the next hour. He knows what is your qadr tomorrow, next week, next month and next year.

And believe this: He knows you yearn to be close to Him. He knows you desire His Paradise and He knows exactly what to give and take away from you; who and what to place on your path and who and what to take away from your path, to take you to Him and His Paradise.

So, there is no need to worry. The sooner you internalise this and etch it onto your heart, the sooner you will find yourself immersed in peace and tranquillity – states that are whispers from Jannah. Peace emerges from the knowledge that you are safe and in the best possible place in what He decrees from His knowledge.

Ibn al-Qayyim said:

> If the servant of Allah knows that He cannot escape nor change the plan of Allah, He will commit all his affairs to Allah and throw himself between His Hands as a humble servant throws himself between the hands of a mighty king who has authority over him – and indeed the servant has no power of his own. When the servant knows all that, he will be relieved from all distress and sadness and will pass the burden to Allah who does not care or get tired. Allah will carry him, and show him kindness and mercy without any tiredness. The servant has paid attention to Allah alone and Allah paid attention to the needs and benefits of his life and emptied his heart from them, and, as a result, his life will be good and his heart will be happy.

Al-Fawaa'id

Now this does not mean we sit idle and do absolutely nothing. We have been created as responsible, proactive humans. We should do everything we can to plan for a better tomorrow. We must tie our camel as we are taught in the following hadith:

> 'O Messenger of Allah, should I tie my camel and trust in Allah, or should I leave her untied and trust in Allah?' The Prophet said, 'Tie her and trust in Allah.'

Sunan Tirmidhi

We should do everything we can. And then we must trust that our plan may not be the best plan. And when He intervenes and diverts us away from the path we embarked upon, or interrupts it, or even turns it upside down – it is then we prove to Him that we are indeed Muslim – a slave who submits to His Will, His plan, His Decree.

Dear reader, as you look back at the past, know this: you cannot fight decree. You cannot change the past. In fact, all that has and has not happened in the past was chosen for you by the One who chose you to exist and be here. Shaykh Ibn Uthaymeen said,

Do not hate a thing which Allah has chosen for you, certainly whatever Allah has chosen for you has a great benefit which you do not know about.

Riyaadh As-Saliheen

As we continue this journey of taqwa – to become conscious of Allah – I invite you to live with the Name and Attribute of Allah, Al-Wakil. Living with Al-Wakil, believing in Him, trusting in Him, is to ask of Him and to trust in His Decree. To have faith that He is the Best Disposer of our affairs and disposes of them perfectly. And often the perfection of how He does that is only fully realised and internalised years later. Remember this: if any other situation was better for you, Allah would have written it so.

I leave you with some final reflections on qadr. The Prophet (ﷺ) said,

Nothing repels the divine decree but supplication.

Sunan Tirmidhi

Shayban Al-Ra'i said to Sufyan:

'Consider O Sufyan, that when Allah does not give you something, it is a form of granting you something. Indeed Allah did not prevent you out of miserliness. He did so out of love for you.'

Ibn al-Jawzi, *Sayd Al-Khater*

Today, as you look back at the qadr of your past, perhaps – just perhaps – all that occurred was preparing you for the very things you have been asking for.

Place your full trust in the Best Disposer of your affairs.

Let Your Heart Ponder . . .

'He whom Allah has predestined to enter Paradise, the reasons which will cause his entrance shall spring from calamities; and he whom Allah has predestined to enter the Hellfire, the reasons which will cause his entrance shall spring from lusts.'

Ibn al-Qayyim

'You are the most precious creature to Allah, so be content with what Allah has decreed for you, because a person who loves never questions or accuses the one he loves. The blessings of Allah upon you in all that He has created for your sake are as clear as daylight; so how could you imagine that He would be neglectful when you are at the root of it all?'

Ibn al-Jawzi, *Kitab Al-Lataif*

Du'a Invitation

Al-Wali, The Protector and Supporter, I hand over myself and my life to You. I do so willingly – full of trust that You will decree what is most certainly best for me. In declaring that there is none worthy of worship except You, I also declare that there is none who can grant what is best and protect me from what is not more than You. I ask You for all that will draw me closer to You. I ask You for that which is good for me in this life and the next. I know that You will give me what I have asked for. I trust fully in that. Increase my trust and reliance upon You.

Journal

1. At this exact moment in my life, I need to entrust to Allah the following . . .

....

....

2. Reflect over your past. What one thing has been granted to you that changed so much for you?

....

....

3. Reflect over your past. What one thing that was not granted to you or taken away from you changed so much for you, for the better?

....

....

4. I need to make changes to my mindset to truly live the rest of my life with full trust that Allah is granting me exactly what I need. These changes are . . .

....

....

My reflections
on the topic of Qadr are . . .

....

....

....

....

....

....

....

....

....

....

....

....

....

DAY 9

Being Tested

The Messenger of Allah (ﷺ) said, 'Take advantage of five before five: your youth before your old age, your health before your illness, your riches before your poverty, your free time before your work, and your life before your death.'

In the days that lead up to the sight of the elegant silver line of the Ramadan new crescent moon, there is a unique feeling in the air. Feelings of anticipation, excitement, relief and hope are felt that this will truly become a transformative month in faith and closeness to Allah ('azza wa jal). The planners come out, dates are bought in bulk and you mentally create images of pure servitude in the early hours of the morning, with heart prostrating in unison with body. You organise your days and nights meticulously, hoping to 'take advantage of five before five'. You make a promise to take better care of your health; better care of your wealth; better management of your time.

You might start the first few days of Ramadan with consistency: regular portion of Qur'an read – check. Sadaqa given – check. Taraweeh prayed – check. And then bam! Something happens that throws you off course and you find yourself struggling to climb back onto the Ramadan-worship wagon.

This is symbolic of what happens to us in life. We may have a long record of ease, joy, happiness and strong faith. And then, being the human beings that we are, we slip into forgetfulness and revert to our old ways.

Then Allah ('azza wa jal) does something. He chooses people. He tests them. He places them in the middle of a storm – not to cause disruption, rather to clear the path ahead. These people come face to face with sudden loss that literally shifts the knowledge of 'take five before five' from the back to the very forefront of the mind. The physical rotation of this important concept is intentional. Only this test will shift it to a position of priority and focus.

For some, it comes in the sudden loss of wealth. For others, they find death right before them in the form of a sudden accident or upon learning of a terminal illness or the worsening of one. For others it is death itself that will be the only means to their awakening to life and all that it means.

Whether your major test occurred in the past or you are currently experiencing it right now, know this: you have been selected and chosen. The initial shock of your loss may have stunned you into silence – you do not know what to do, what to say or how to move forward in your life. And that is okay – you are human. You are allowed to grieve. Feel that loss deeply. Ride its waves. In fact, be the wave and allow yourself to move and crash as you need to. It is all right.

Then, when you are ready, sit still and internalise this: you have been chosen. You have been selected by the Owner of all that exists to become hyper aware, to take heed, to change, to act differently. And that is a beautiful divine gift. You have been invited to consciousness of Allah, which produces consciousness in life.

Take five before five is advice to the masses. Being tested with sudden loss that awakens your soul to that which is important is a gift given to a selected few by the Lord of the Heavens.

I invite you to look back at the major tests of your life. And please do so from a healthy distance.

As I look back at my own past, there have been many little tests along the way but there have been three major ones that have brought me to my knees and rocked me to my core. For privacy's sake, I will not go into the details of those tests – maybe

I will one day when I am at a greater stage of vulnerability, perhaps in a memoir. For now, I can tell you they were tests in my childhood, and through illness and betrayal.

During the days of one of the aforementioned storms, I was reading the Qur'an in a state of utter desperation. You know, that feeling when you're in such agony, yearning for a way out – desperate to not feel the way you do, you pick up the Qur'an hoping to find a verse that fills the cracks in your heart with a soothing balm. In such a state, I wrote the following:

I've come across this verse many times but today one word stood out for me . . .

Or did you expect to enter the Garden (of Paradise) before the like of (the trials that befell) those who passed on before you had befallen you? Misery and adversity afflicted them, and they were shaken as with an earthquake, until the Messenger and those who believed with him would say, "When is Allah's support (coming)?" Undoubtedly, Allah's support is indeed near.

Surah Baqarah 2:214

The word that stood out was 'zulzilu' which is translated as 'shaken'. With a basic level of Arabic, one can see it is from the same root as zilzalah, meaning earthquake.

When we're tested, we are so violently shaken within that, like the earth, we feel split open; ripped apart. We experience a primary pain – the pain of our tests. And sometimes experience a secondary pain: the pain of guilt and frustration that our internal earthquake equates to weak faith.

We are human and we are Muslim. Let me say that again: we are human and we are Muslim. Your internal turmoil is natural and experienced by the strongest of believers. There is nothing to feel guilty about. We are not angels, unshaken by our tests.

Anyone who has experienced a real earthquake (and I'm one of them) will tell you the fear and temporary loss of control of themselves as they're shaken. Realise your temporary internal earthquake is simply the colliding of your human 'plates'. Why add to your burden by burdening your soul with thoughts that you're a weak Muslim?

I have witnessed people screaming and crying out to Allah at the onset of an earthquake. I, myself, remember my first earthquake in the city of Algiers. I was awoken from my sleep by a loud thudding sound I had never heard before. As my room shook from side to side all I could repeatedly say was, 'Ya Allah, ya Allah.'

When you are shaken, turn to Him. Who else can truly help you at the onset of an earthquake except Him?

As the ayah (verse) ends, remember this: without doubt, and with full faith and certainty, know that the Help of Allah is near.

You may be wondering why I have invited you to recall your most difficult test to date. Why now in Ramadan? Because lessons from the past can transform our present and future.

A number of years ago, I felt that I had a great balance between my home and work life. I was running my own charity, home-educating my children, getting ready to move to another country and my business was doing well, Alhamdulillah. As an organised person, I had it all together and life was good, Alhamdulillah.

I was then hit with the biggest test of my life. This test turned my internal and external life upside down. Unknown to the world who still perceived 'Aliyah Umm Raiyaan' as having it all together, underneath I was struggling. In between struggling to survive on a daily basis, I found it so very hard to continue with all of my various responsibilities. I was in the middle of teaching a course that I had the sole responsibility to see through to the end. My children needed me more than ever after our move from the UK to North Africa. Cooking, cleaning, study, work plus this major test took its toll. And yet, the soldier in me continued to work, to teach and to tend to my responsibilities but without the passion and attention I would normally give to these. I was just about able to do the basics in every area of my life.

There are lessons in the major tests we have encountered in life that we need as we look to become more present and mindful. Two of them, I would like to share with you.

The first is in the very beliefs that we hold. As you consider the major tests of your past, what limiting beliefs did you have about your test and/or your ability to get through them?

The limiting belief I had during my hardest test was that it would never end and that Allah had forsaken me. I was drowning in despair. I now know for certainty that this was all due to my perception and nothing to do with Allah at all.

It is very normal to feel the struggle during a test and to feel so immersed and overwhelmed with it all that you cannot see the wood for the trees. It is called being human. It is okay to have your down days. It is also okay to feel both mentally and physically weaker than usual, as well as to question and doubt. Allah wants us to pass through our test knowing that He sees us and what we are going through. We are not alone. With this, our tests that are accompanied by weakness, doubt and struggles are now perceived with the knowledge that He is looking at us intently and that He wants us to walk through this test with Him. And He really is – He is with us through it all.

I have learnt it is okay to have moments of being very human with our trials and difficulties. And it is important to know Allah understands that and wants for us to be human with Him. And that is when and where the solutions are found and peace descends.

When Allah granted me the end of my test, I was so overjoyed and so full of energy. The difference in how I felt was like night and day. I felt like I could take on the world again. And in some ways that is what I did. The things I had stopped during my time of difficulty, I restarted. On top of that, I started new things. For nearly two years, I had stopped taking on clients, stopped teaching courses; I began anew. Solace UK, the charity I founded emerged once again and the team did so much in that year that I felt full of joy to be serving again. I was back.

In hindsight, I realised that I made a mistake. A doctor encourages us to rest after a period of illness; to regain our strength. When we are exhausted, the body shuts down, forcing us to sleep so that we are ready and rejuvenated for a new day. Similarly, after difficulty, there is a time of stillness and rest that is required for us to continue with life as stronger individuals, but is often ignored.

I mistook the sudden surge of energy to mean a new lease of life. That surge was simply the difference between choppy and still waters. The contrast was so sudden that all I could see were calm waters, forgetting the destruction of turbulent crashing waves I had been immersed in. And the required time to adjust to the new state of the water.

Upon reflection, I now realise that immediately after the test I needed time to rest; this was to occur from within. Though the waters were now calm and still, though the test was over, I needed that time to adjust to my new state of stability.

We seem to think that the passing of a test means we now have to revert to an autopilot mode. That we now need to and are able to become more and do more and achieve more. The calm waters often deceive us into thinking we can now attempt the hard task of fishing when, just before, we were drowning.

Take time out after being tested. Rest. Recover. Be still. Enjoy the calm. Do just the basics and gather your strength again for the next chapter of your life.

As a final thought on the really difficult tests, I read a quote by the Australian activist Christine Caine that summarises it perfectly:

When you're in a dark place, you sometimes tend to think you've been buried. Perhaps you've been planted. Bloom.

When your eyes are not seeing what Allah wants you to see, He will often test you to the point of catastrophe, until not only do your physical eyes see it, but the eyes of your soul see it too.

There is always purpose in your major trials.

Let Your Heart Ponder . . .

'Sa'd ibn Abi Waqqas reported: I said, "O Messenger of Allah, which people are tested most severely?" The Messenger of Allah (ﷺ) said, "They are the Prophets, then the next best, then the next best. A man is put to trial according to his religion. If he is firm in his religion, his trials will be more severe. If he is weak in his religion, he is put to trial according to his strength in religion. The servant will continue to be put to trial until he is left walking upon the earth without any sin."'

Sunan Tirmidhi

Du'a Invitation

Al-Qarib, The One who is Close, You said, 'I am as My servant expects of Me and I am with him as he remembers Me. If he remembers Me in himself, I will remember him in Myself. If he mentions Me in a gathering, I will mention him in a greater gathering. When he draws near Me by the span of his hand, I draw near him by the length of a cubit. When he draws near Me by the length of a cubit, I draw near him by the length of a fathom. When he comes to Me walking, I come to him running.'

I am Your servant who believes You have tested me severely because You love me and wish to purify me. In the tests that have passed, I choose to perceive them in light of who You are – Loving, Kind, Merciful. You placed my tests on my path – not to break me. You placed them on my path – to make me. I ask You for ease. And should You decide to test me in the future, I pledge to ride the storms with You. All I need to do is move towards You and You will come to me at speed. Al-Hakim, The Most Wise, increase my wisdom to see the lessons you want me to learn. My Lord, do not test me in my faith. Allow my trials to transform my faith.

Journal

1. Write down the three major tests you have experienced to date.

....

....

2. How have they changed your life for the better?

....

....

3. How specifically did they change your relationship with Allah?

....

....

4. With a bird's-eye view of your life, what might have been the wisdom behind these tests?

....

....

5. I take the following two lessons and I move forward into my life . . .

....

....

**My reflections
on the topic of
Being Tested are . . .**

DAY 10

Allah, I Need to Talk to You about My Past

I remember standing on the blue deck of the ferry on my way to Algeria. It had been a long trip, driving from South London with our seven-seater silver Toyota Previa, packed to the ceiling with books, kitchenware, clothes and toys. It had been an arduous task to decide what to take with us and what to sell or throw away. We left nothing behind.

First, we drove to Folkestone, then through the Eurotunnel to Calais and began the long road journey to Marseille in the South of France. Boarding the *Tariq bin Ziyad* ferry to Algiers was the final stretch. It was an overnight crossing. When I awoke in the oak-furnished cabin, reminiscent of the 1950s, I got dressed and climbed the stairs to the open top deck. The morning was so fresh – seagulls flew above and in the distance I could see land.

The journey of packing up, saying our goodbyes and travelling from the UK to Europe and now to the very northern tip of Africa produced a mix of emotions from within.

At that very moment, I spoke to my Lord and said,

Allah, here I am. You are my Lord – Alone with no
partners. I am Your servant. I praise You for who You are.
I have left what is familiar for Your Sake. Thank You for
all You have given to us. Thank You for all that You have
blessed me with. Thank You for all the people,
experiences, provision that I enjoyed in the UK. Thank
You for the lessons and the growth. Forgive me for my
shortcomings. Wipe away my sins for You have promised
hijrah (emigration to a Muslim country) is a means to
being forgiven. My Lord, I am nervous. I don't know
what the future holds. As I approach the land of Algiers,
I ask You to grant my family the best of faith,
experiences and people that lead us to You.

I cried and the tears kept falling. I was flooded with memories
of the past – myself as a non-Muslim teenager, fun times,
embracing Islam, marriage, the birth of my children, graduating
as a mature student while mothering three children, home-
educating, community picnics, the launch of Solace UK – a registered charity I founded that supports Muslim revert women in
difficulty. Faces of loved ones passed by in my mind like a slide-
show. It was a bittersweet moment.

The first third of Ramadan will soon pass us by. This is how
quickly our life passes on. Gone. Never to return. We have no
way of revisiting the last ten days and changing them to make a
difference to our Ramadan, just as we have no way of revisiting
and changing the days of our past to make a difference to our
life. We can only do so by applying their lessons to today.

Through reflection, we have spent ten days healing from our
past. We have begun the journey of letting go of all that which
is weighing us down on this journey of taqwa. We have begun
to discover treasures in lessons that can help us as we continue
that journey.

It is time to talk to Allah:

Allah,

All praise and glory is for You Alone. You are the Light of the Heavens and Earth. You are indeed the Most Great. There is no might and no power except with You. You are the Knower of the unseen. You are the Most Merciful, the Perfect One, the Bestower of Faith, Exalted in Might. You are my Creator. You fashioned me. You are Most Wise. To You belong the Most Beautiful Names.

My Lord, have mercy upon Muhammad (ﷺ) and send peace upon him.

You have told me, 'I have not created jinn or man, except to worship Me.' I am here, breathing and living to worship You. This is my purpose. I came from You and I will return to You. In my five daily prayers, I declare Your Oneness – that none has the right to be worshipped except You. Just as I make that declaration, I declare to You that I am making a choice to make You a priority above all else.

You have not created me to simply float through life. You have created me to live life with my destination in front of me at all times.

Allah, you know my life is hectic. There is so much to do, all day, every day. So many people need me. There are so many demands on my time.

But with my purpose at the forefront of my mind, I know how important it is to take time out to be silent, still and reflect. In Your creation, You have shown me that there are alternations between day and night and similarly I must, on this journey to You, alternate between busyness and reflection.

O Allah, so much has happened in my life. I choose to see every experience as a teacher – providing me with tailor-made lessons just for me. My Most Generous Lord, You have brought lessons for me to learn. And for that I am ever grateful. I commit to being a responsible student who takes those lessons and learns. I am a student who will make mistakes. I'll forget what You have taught me. I'll remember and then I will make mistakes again. I ask You for Your patience and yet I need not ask, for You are The Most Patient.

Allah, guide my mind and heart – sharpen them to take the lessons in so that I remain on the path to You and Your Jannah.

And when I get the lessons, when I really get them – I know it is only because You allowed me to, because of Your love for me. I feel shy when I acknowledge Your love for me. For You are the Lord of everyone and everything and yet, You love me – I am but a speck in the universe. Your Love does not diminish with my weaknesses or mistakes. It does not diminish with my forgetfulness. You are forever with me watching me – a second is never missed. Even when I am asleep, Your Loving Gaze is upon me, looking at me intently. What greater love is there than a love where You, my Beloved looks upon Your servant and slave.

O Allah, the love I experience with You and from You is ever so sweet. Strengthen me to protect it at all costs.

When I look back at my past, I haven't valued Your Love as much as I should have. Perhaps it is because I did not know how truly valuable Your Love is. But I do now. I need You so very much. So place in my heart a sensor that goes off at anything that will takes me away from You. And place another sensor in my heart that goes off at anything that will increase my love for You and Your love for me.

I am a bird flying to you with wings of fear and hope. When I veer towards one, straighten my wings, ya Rabbi. Guide my flight.

I trust you fully for everything You have given and taken away from me. I trust what You have written for me because I know You. You are the Lord who created me with love and wishes for me to permanently exist in peace, joy and love. So I know anything that has happened in my past is from a place of love – best for me in every single way.

I am a grateful servant. I thank You for my health, my wealth and the people in my life. I thank You for Giving and Withholding at exactly the right time. I thank You for my tests, which were a means towards certain opportunities and meeting people that would be essential on my journey. I thank You for my faith. I thank You for giving me the opportunity to look back, take lessons and apply them to my future.

I thank You for my belief.

I am a grateful servant today and tomorrow I may forget to thank You. When I forget, I ask You to pardon me and guide me.

I'm ready, ya Rabbi. I am ready to let go of anything that will not aid me on my path of taqwa. I am ready to carry everything that will. I desire to be near You. I am ready to do everything in the present – to live a truly God-conscious life.

Go back to the reflections on the topics
that you journaled about at the end of the previous
nine chapters. Read over them. Now pen your own
private thoughts about your past to the One
who Listens, Allah.

PART 2:

Journeying to Allah with Presence

'The East and the West belong to Allah, so wherever you turn, Allah's Presence will be there. Indeed Allah is Boundlessly Vast, the Knowing.'

Surah Baqarah 2:115

This current page of this chapter of your life is the most important one.

Dear reader, I invite you to be present.

DAY 11

Presence

A white-beaked duck has just nose-dived into the lake before me, leaving circular ripples as it disappears. An older lady has just walked passed me, looking trendy in a peach shirt, blue gilet and trainers. The fountain is shooting up clouds of water. To the right, under umbrellas of newly turned yellow leaves as the trees submit to the season of autumn, a man is taking a photo of the lake. And to my left, a mother peers into a grey pushchair, pulling funny faces at her little one. I can hear the footsteps behind me accompanied by a chorus of heavy breaths as runners complete their laps of the park. The whizz of electric bikes fades after they pass me by. An orchestra of birds tweeting, ducks quacking, the sound of the fountain before me, human chatter of different languages and cars driving by makes me feel at home in London.

The wooden worn-out planks of the bench that I am sitting on look so old, yet are secure enough to make me feel stable. I am sat while tiptoeing as I balance my laptop on my knees, conscious that I am taking a risk – writing here on my laptop in the heart of an East London park.

There was a whiff just now that smelt like perfume – there it is again. I cannot see any flowers so I wonder where the scent is coming from. The air is warm but every so often it bites on this late summer's day, causing me to pull my red cardigan tight around me. And just as I have written this, there is a wind that tells me, 'Don't be fooled, autumn is closer than you realise – I am on my way.'

I can still taste the remnants of the chocolate that I ate as I parked my car by the roadside.

I sit here and I am breathing slowly. I feel calm. I feel at peace. I feel present.

This is presence. To offer yourself to your senses as they take in the world.

Today, as we start the second third of Ramadan, I could not start this chapter by recounting a story from my past. The only way for me to tell you about presence was to take myself where I could be present.

And I have a confession to make. All day I have tried to write this chapter. It is currently 6.25pm. I tried to fit it in while doing other work, washing last night's fajita pan, teaching math to my nine-year-old, checking that my twelve-year-old was signed into his online class, calling my older son, responding to WhatsApp messages from my eldest to confirm whether she had forgotten her laptop at home. I could not write about presence when I was far from it – distracted by the ongoing demands of life. It frustrated me. All I wanted was to be present enough to write about presence.

Some days are just like that – when you need to be present, you feel yourself taken away from the norm and unable to just soak in the simplistic wonders your senses provide you.

As I look upon this beautiful view of seagulls flying overhead, ducks mind their own business as they paddle in the water, I feel grounded. I am here.

I just took a deep breath. Finally, I am ready to write.

We are all on this intense and interesting journey of life – despite all its twists and turns, ups and downs and even ugliness, it is the best of journeys because it leads us to the Best of all Destinations. And while our eyes are fixed on the destination, we cannot forego the journey of what we see and can learn from along the way. Your journey is made up of millions of moments. I realised this as I watched people of different colours, ages, heights, sizes and religions walk past me in front of the lake. Despite our apparent differences, we are all the same. We are all His Creation. We all came from Him and we are all going to return to Him. And in between coming from Him and returning to Him, we are souls living out moments. The past moment is no more. The future moment has not occurred. All we have right now is the present moment.

As we enter the second third of Ramadan, knowing how truly precious these Ramadan days are in spirituality and reward, we can see how our moments in these remaining days are so very precious.

You have one chance at this dunya. Only one chance. The moments in the days of your life are all that you have. Choosing how present you are in as many moments as you can creates a meaningful life.

In these blessed days and nights, I encourage you to choose how you live from one moment to the next.

Let us try it right now. Where are you right now? Look around you. What or who is in your vicinity? Take it all in. What are you seeing? What can you hear? What can you smell, taste and feel? This is all you have right now. Relax your shoulders, breathe in deeply – exhale. Breathe in and exhale again – this time really slowly. Now, smile.

As you take in your surroundings in this very moment – whether you are sitting, standing or lying down – journey with me.

Look around you and focus on what you can see. Thank Allah for blessing you with eyes that take in shape, form and colour. Feel the gratitude in your heart for everything that is falling into your vision that He has blessed you with. Feel your lips part as you whisper, 'Alhamdulillah (all praise and thanks are due to Allah).'

Now shift your awareness to the soundwaves entering your ears. Perhaps you are sat in silence. If so, notice the sounds far away or simply focus on the sound of silence and feel still within it. Perhaps there are a lot of sounds around you – take them all in. Are there voices of people you have been blessed with? Are there noises belonging to things you use to make life easier, for study, work or even play? As I write this, I can hear the clicks as my fingers press down on the keys and I am grateful to Allah for my laptop and the opportunity to write this book. And in this very moment, I am reminded of a du'a I made as I made the largest purchase of my life – this MacBook Air in 2018 – 'Oh Allah, let me use it for Your sake.' Subhana'Allah, He knew then the purpose for which it would be used.

Is there anything you can smell or taste? What was the last thing you ate or drank? Your Lord continues to provide for you, nourish and sustain you regardless of how much or how little you do for Him.

Right now, focus on the ground beneath your feet. In fact, feel your feet in your shoes, in your socks, or experience the feeling of them exposed to the air. Or your hands if they are holding this book. What does it feel like to grasp its covers? Your Lord has provided you with the ability to feel physically and emotionally. He has granted you the experience of feeling connected to the world and all that it contains, and having a spiritual connection to Him.

This is your life. Moments. With Allah intimately and intentionally watching each and every one.

Focus just on the here and now. It does not matter who you were moments before. You are a servant of Allah who, right now, acknowledges His Guidance and Blessings. In fact, your ability to see, hear, smell, taste and touch are blessings.

Connecting to our present moments is crucial on this journey. By connecting to our present, we are able to see blessings that require thanks, feelings that require help and direction, thoughts that require rewiring, and dreams that require hope.

Every single moment can be connected to Allah – and if this is not the meaning of taqwa, I do not know what is.

Today, I had to take myself to the park to get myself into a more present state. When life is so full and busy, I find that I have to every so often prioritise my soul by immersing it in something connected to nature in order to be present and reconnect with the Creator. I once heard a speaker say, 'Every so often, your heart needs to see greenery.' He could not be more right.

Sometimes, though, I find that I need not remove myself intentionally to be present. Sometimes presence can be achieved in the mundane moments of life. Feeling the soap escape the sponge as I wash the dishes. Looking at the clouds in the sky as I walk to the tube station. Focusing on the coolness of water as it runs down my throat. Enjoying the touch of a hand, melting into an embrace or really taking in a person's smile. All of these things while getting on with the daily grind of life.

Either consciously taking yourself away to have time to be present or simply focusing on being present in your normal everyday moments is about creating a meaningful life. We are not robots. We are not empty shells. We are souls who need connection to spiritually survive and thrive. And we can do so easily through presence.

The path of taqwa entails having as much consciousness of Him as is possible in each moment of your life, knowing that this may be your very last. Taqwa is not a thing of the past or the future. Taqwa is in the here and now – a journey steeped in presence. You are either journeying with God-consciousness or you are not. It is either happening or it is not. And the great thing is, you can choose to do so at any time that you wish. It is a simple choice.

The Prophet (ﷺ) said,

Verily, the religion is easy and no one burdens himself in religion but that it overwhelms him. Follow the right course, seek closeness to Allah, give glad tidings, and seek help for worship in the morning and evening and a part of the night.

Bukhari

Approaching taqwa in this way, it does not matter where you are in your Qur'an reading on this eleventh day of Ramadan. It does not matter if you have been held back from worship due to illness, sadness, difficulty or even just not feeling it. Taqwa is an invitation to all and you can respond to that invitation right now by being conscious of who your Lord is in the moments of your life. And this is where the mundane becomes worship. This is how you can truly value time – not through schedules, checklists or quantity. Rather do everything – whether worship or ordinary tasks – with presence of heart and faith, connecting to your moments and connecting those moments to Him.

And if your worship has increased, Alhamdulillah, and you are praying more, remembering Him more and giving more, ensure that you are fully present in those acts of ibadah (worship) – focusing on what your limbs are doing, your heart is uttering and your heart is feeling – for all of this was only possible by His Love and Permission.

Allah ('azza wa jal) has made this journey to Him easy because He really does want Jannah for you. Reflect on that.

Be present.

Let Your Heart Ponder . . .

'Whatever matter you are dealing with, and whatever part of the Qur'an you are reciting and whatever you are doing, We are witnessing what you are doing.'

Surah Yunus, 10:61

Du'a Invitation

Ya Al-Hayy Al-Qayyum, The Living, The Sustainer, help me be here. Guide me to disconnect in order to connect. I thank You for my faculties and senses. I thank You for what they take in every single day. I thank You for placing people and experiences in my life to teach me to be present. Help me become more present. Allow my eyes to see what is, instead of focusing on what I hope for there to be. Assist me in leading a life where I find You everywhere – in all my moments.

Journal

1. I am often distracted by . . .

....

....

....

2. These distractions are impacting my wellbeing and relationships with others and myself in the following ways . . .

....

....

....

3. I can do the following to become more present in my life . . .

....

....

....

4. Right now, I can see, hear, smell, taste and touch the following . . .

....

....

....

**My reflections
on the topic of Presence are . . .**

DAY 12

Last Day

'Please remember me and my family in your du'a. Losing my battle with Covid-19 at hospital at the moment. It's been two weeks. Get a bad day then a good day. Then I think of my children. The hardest bit is to be completely isolated from loved ones. Someone to put their hand on your forehead and make du'a for you.'

These were the last words I received from my dear beloved friend Mona Mustafa, who tragically died five days later.

Mona was a daughter, sister, wife and mother of five children. She worked with refugees. She was a light wherever she went. Her smile and laughter were contagious and she gave the best hugs. Scrolling through my phone, with her profile picture now missing, it is still hard to imagine she is no longer here.

She had plans. In October 2019 she told me she had started her Masters and asked me to assist her with her motivation and academic writing. We met in November and got to some root issues that were causing her to experience imposter syndrome, blocking her natural ability to write academically and well.

She never got to finish her Masters. Neither of us knew at the time that only five months later she would leave this world and return to her Lord.

Standing by her grave two months later was hard. But it was necessary. At the time, there was no headstone – just a heap of earth rubble and a simple wooden piece of wood that had been placed temporarily into the earth with her row, grave number and name written in black marker pen.

I stood there looking down at the pile of earth and imagined her covered in her white shroud beneath and knew that one day someone too will be standing over me. She had her last day in this world. My mind drifted: 'In what circumstances will I be in on my last day?'

The irony of Ramadan is that we literally count the days. The day the moon is sighted. Whether there will be twenty-nine or thirty days. The twentieth day that signals the last ten nights of Ramadan. The odd nights of the last ten. And finally, the nights we look for the moon of the month of Shawaal, which ends Ramadan and allows us to enjoy the day of Eid.

All these days – each with their own significance. And yet only one day really matters: today. Today is all that matters because there is absolutely no guarantee of there being a tomorrow.

Abdul Malik Clare said,

> Don't wait to get old to worship Allah. If today is your last day, you are old already.
>
> B. B. Abdullah, *Timeless Seeds of Advice*

Mona died on 11 April 2020. Ramadan that year began on 23 April 2020.

There is no guarantee of anything in this life except this: just as we all had our birth day, we are guaranteed to have our last day.

Yesterday we initiated a relationship with presence. Today, I invite you to take that one step further and do what the Messenger of Allah advised us:

> Allah's Messenger (ﷺ) took hold of my shoulders and said, 'Be in this world as if you were a stranger or a passing traveller.' And Ibn 'Umar used to say, 'If you survive till the evening, do not expect to live till the morning, and if you survive till the morning, do not

expect to live till the evening, and take from your health for your sickness, and take from your life for your death.'

Bukhari

In the first ten days of this book, there was an invitation to change your mindset and heart. There was an invitation to heal and heed lessons. Now, I invite you to take all of the lessons and growth of your past and apply it to today with the following words of al-Hasan al-Basri as a reminder for your soul:

I have never regretted something; except that I regretted a day, that the sun had set; in which my life span decreased (in days) but my (good) deeds did not increase (in number).

Hifdh al-Waqt fi Ramadan

Your last day, which can occur at any time that has already been predestined, is a prelude to the last leg of the journey of your soul. Your body will be washed. It will be shrouded. It will be prayed over. And as you are carried to your new home, you take nothing with you except how you spent the moments of your life.

With this in mind, and in a month where good deeds are multiplied, I invite you to incorporate the following awareness into every single day, knowing it may be your last; for:

The Messenger of Allah (ﷺ) said, 'The first action for which a servant of Allah will be held accountable on the Day of Resurrection will be his prayers. If they are in order, he will have prospered and succeeded. If they are lacking, he will have failed and lost. If there is something defective in his obligatory prayers, then the Almighty Lord will say: See if My servant has any voluntary prayers that can complete what is insufficient in his obligatory prayers. The rest of his deeds will be judged the same way.'

Sunan Tirmidhi

What I love about this hadith is that we can all find our place therein. Dear reader, if you are not praying, you can begin. If you are praying and your five daily prayers are lacking in timing and presence, you can compensate through voluntary prayers. If you offer both, you can increase in khushoo (focus in prayer).

Regardless of which of the above categories you fall into, it is time to prioritise your salah (five daily prayers) on this journey of taqwa. It is the first thing you will be judged upon; in the words of the companion of the Prophet, Mu'adh bin Jabal, when advising his son:

> My son! Pray the prayer of the one who is leaving, and realise that you might not be able to pray ever again. And know, my son, the believer dies between two good deeds; one he performed and one he intended to perform (later).

Ibn al-Jawzi, Sifat as Safwah

Absolutely everything else is secondary. Remember that.

Next is the practice of remembrance in the morning and evening. To quote the author Tim Ferris, 'If you win the morning, you win the day.' The morning and evening adhkaar (morning and evening prayer and remembrance) are indicative of how important it is to start and end our day correctly. Knowing that we could die at any given moment in the day, we are taught to do the dhikr (remembrances of Allah), du'a and affirmation each morning and evening so that our days are blessed – and also so that the last things we say before we start our day or end it are related to our journey of taqwa and our path to Him. Consider downloading an app where you can find the morning and evening adhkaar. Do not simply recite the Arabic or just read a translation in your mother tongue. Pay attention to the meaning. Be present with the words and then go about your day and, before you tire, bid it farewell with these remembrances.

Every day, maximise on the intentions you set with the moments you have. Wherever possible, have the intention of making this moment a means to Allah. Increase your intention – and have multiple intentions. The Messenger of Allah (ﷺ) said,

> Verily, deeds are only with intentions and every person will have only what they intended. Whoever emigrated to Allah and His Messenger, his emigration is for Allah and His Messenger. Whoever emigrated to get something in the world or to marry a woman, his emigration is for that to which he emigrated.

> Bukhari and Muslim

In this way, you are making each moment a means of reward, which will be the only possession you take with you after you leave this world.

A suggestion is to use the routine of salah to pause five times a day, consciously breaking away from whatever you are doing and saying, 'Allah, I love you more than what I was doing.' Take this a step further and attach good deeds to your routine of the five daily prayers. It may be a call with the intention of uphold-ing the ties of kinship. A quick £2 sadaqa donation. A smile. A kind word. Helping someone and doing what is most beloved to Allah of all good deeds: making another Muslim happy. It is almost like using the five daily prayers as alarms to do good. With Fajr prayer as the first prayer, Dhur as the 'lunchtime' prayer, Asr as the early evening prayer, Maghrib as the 'sunset' prayer and Isha as the last prayer – doing good at these times will mean you have done something to aid you on your journey towards Him. For the truth is that you will die either at the time of a prayer or certainly between two prayers. So make the most of this five-prayer routine.

The next recommendation can be found in the words of the scholar Ibn Taymiyyah, who wrote, 'Dhikr is to the heart what water is to a fish, see what happens when a fish is taken out of water.' Remembrance of Allah prevents a death before death. Use at least some of the gaps in time – waiting for the bus, the hour spent at the supermarket, the fifteen minutes washing the dishes or waiting for the lecturer to turn up or a work meeting – in reflection on Allah.

Istighfaar – the act of seeking forgiveness from Allah – provides sustenance (Surah 71 in the Qur'an: verses 10–12). Istighfaar opens the door of mercy (15:49). Istighfaar removes stress and anxiety. It is the eraser of sins (16:119). Istighfaar leads to a granted du'a (38:55). Look up these verses.

Implementing the above suggestions, each and every day – which may well be your last – you will have done your best with the first deed of salah, which will be looked upon first. You will have enveloped yourself in asking good for yourself in this life and the next. You will have maximised on as many moments as possible through multiple intentions. You will have spaced out good deeds throughout the day. And in between all of this you will have used your time to remember your Lord – reminding yourself that if you are blessed with life tomorrow, because you came from Him and will return to Him, it will be a blessing to be able to repeat all of this again.

Live each day
ready to meet Allah.

Let Your Heart Ponder . . .

'If you want to know your value with your Lord,
look to how he is using you and what actions he
has kept you busy with.'

Ibn al-Jawzi

'. . . whoever is mindful of Allah – He will make for
him a way out (of every difficulty) and will provide
for him from where he never expects, and whoever
places his trust in Allah – He will suffice him. Allah
shall indeed conclude His decreed matters; Allah
has set a due measure for everything.

Surah At-Talaq 65:2–3

Du'a Invitation

Ash-Shakir, The Recogniser and Rewarder of good, make my
last day my best day. Make it my best day in matters of my faith,
my good deeds, my level of repentance and my Love for You.
Take me upon the best of my deeds. I ask You for a good end to
my life.

Journal

1. Close your eyes and imagine tomorrow is your last day. What would you need to do as an absolute top priority? Write this down. Ask Allah for help.

....

....

....

2. Now, go do those things.

....

....

....

3. Which of your affairs do you need to rectify?

....

....

4. Make a list of simple good deeds you can do at the time of prayer. Save them on your phone for easy access.

....

....

**My reflections
on the topic of a Last Day are . . .**

DAY 13

Ihsaan

One Ramadan, my husband and I intended to treat ourselves by breaking our daily fast with iftar (the post-dusk meal) in a restaurant. We drove to Stoke Newington where countless Turkish restaurants and their piping hot grills were waiting for us. We parked the car and decided to pray in Azizye Mosque and then find somewhere to eat. After finishing salah, we went to get a table at the Azizye restaurant, to be told by the tired Turkish waiter that they were fully booked and had no space for the next ninety minutes.

Hungry and disheartened, as we had been looking forward to this iftar for some time, we walked out of the restaurant's side door. Immediately a man approached us carrying blue plastic bags – the kind that are handed to you after buying meat in a halal butcher shop. He had at least five on each arm, each bag tied by its handles.

'Assalamu alaikum, please,' he said putting the bags down and handing us two.

'No brother, it's okay – we came to have iftar,' my husband said, pointing at the Azizye restaurant sign situated underneath the mosque.

The brother insisted we take the bags and would not take no for an answer. He must have been in his mid-thirties. Simply dressed. Maybe of Pakistani or Afghani origin.

We reluctantly took the bags from our fellow Muslim brother, thanked him and walked out of the masjid (mosque) towards the car. We exchanged a look that translated into, 'What do we

117

do now?' Both of us had so been looking forward to having our iftar together at this restaurant. And now we had been given food which would in no way resemble the meal we had been looking forward to.

I broke the silence and said, 'I'm so hungry and this is qadr. Let's just eat.' We climbed into the back of the car and opened the bags.

In those simple plastic bags were a large container, a small container, a zip-locked bag, water, juice and fruit. Opening the large container, we found at least two large pieces of chicken and spiced rice. The salad consisted of olives, peppers, salad, tomatoes and cucumber. But what amazed me was the zip-locked bag. It contained salt, pepper, dressing for the salad, and each piece of cutlery had been hand-wrapped, the napkins folded meticulously. There were also biscuits, tea and sugar. These items were packed with the intention to give someone a perfectly thought-out meal. I find it hard to articulate the beautiful way in which this complimentary iftar meal had been put together and offered to us.

This was not just the act of a fellow Muslim who wanted the reward of feeding the fasting in the way that the Prophet (ﷺ) described:

> Whoever helps break the fast of a fasting person, he will
> have the same reward as him without decreasing
> anything from the reward of the fasting person.

Sunan Tirmidhi

This blue bag was evident of the man's ihsaan (the state of worshipping Allah as though you see Him and though you cannot see Him, knowing He sees you) – his wanting to feed another Muslim with the hope of it being accepted as a deed from a Muhsin (one who aims to achieve the state of ihsaan). Attention had been paid to the fine details. The one receiving the bag may have been so consumed by fulfilling their hunger that they may have not been able to pay attention to the ihsaan of this meal. But as with anything done with ihsaan, it was not about them. All of it is done for the Lord of the Worlds.

God consciousness is the journey of moving from being a Muslim – one who submits in action – to a Mu'min – one who submits in action and becomes a true believer in faith – to a Muhsin(a) – one who finds Him in all moments and experiences, passing through them as though they see Allah. This believer knows that they cannot see Allah but has certitude that He certainly sees them. And this completely transforms their present.

What this Muslim did may seem almost insane. Who would go to such lengths for another person, especially when it is, in fact, so easy to do the bare minimum? Ihsaan is a shift in performing at a minimum level to the maximum level – doing so privately, in such a secret way – that it can only be for Allah.

Ihsaan is born from taqwa. The more conscious we become of Allah in the present, the more we seek Him in the small things and wish to make the small things excellent for His Sake alone. Consciousness of Allah makes you aware that you are in a temporary realm travelling to the permanent realm. Consciousness of Allah gives you a deep awareness of all that He is – through His Beautiful Names and Attributes and all that He does for you every single day. Consciousness of Allah fills you with gratitude, hope and peace. Consciousness of Allah drives you. Oh, does it drive you! The more conscious you become of Allah, the more conscious you become of loving Him and wanting to be close to Him in this life and the next. And that drives you to worship Him with ihsaan – in the faraa'id (obligatory acts of worship) and the nawaafil (recommended acts of worship). You end up falling in love with the nawaafil because it is those deeds that lead you to His Love.

Now I need to repeat something here that I have mentioned above: you are only human. Your life will fluctuate between being a Muslim, a Mu'min and a Muhsin. You are not expected to live as a Muhsin all the time. Perfectionism is an issue because it does not exist. It only exists with Allah ('azza wa jal). And so the path to try to achieve perfectionism will always be ridden with problems – mainly for yourself.

What we want to have and what naturally occurs when we embark upon the path to taqwa is a yearning to be of the muhsineen. And who are the muhsineen? The muhsineen, due to their level of consciousness of God, are lovers of Allah. And so they naturally develop a heightened awareness of their intentions, wanting to make everything a means to Allah – and executing that with as much excellence as possible.

Your yearning is most precious. As the Prophet (ﷺ) said:

> A Bedouin asked the Messenger of Allah (ﷺ), 'When is the Hour?' The Prophet said, 'What have you prepared for it?' The man said, 'Love for Allah and his Messenger.' The Prophet said, 'You will be with those whom you love.'
>
> Bukhari and Muslim

So, with all your imperfections – yearn away. Yearn to be a Muhsin. Yearn to perform deeds with excellence. For you will be with your Lord whom you yearn for and love. And remember that your intentions with Allah are never wasted:

> Allah's Messenger (ﷺ) said that Allah, the Glorious, said: 'Verily, Allah has ordered that the good and the bad deeds be written down. Then He explained it clearly how (to write): He who intends to do a good deed but he does not do it, then Allah records it for him as a full good deed, but if he carries out his intention, then Allah the Exalted writes it down for him as from ten to seven hundred folds, and even more. But if he

intends to do an evil act and has not done it, then Allah writes it down for him as a full good deed, but if he intends it and has done it, Allah writes it down as one bad deed.'

Bukhari and Muslim

On this thirteenth day of Ramadan, having explored the importance of being present, conscious that each day could be our last, it is now important to set your aims high with the lofty goal of ihsaan. The Prophet (ﷺ) taught us to aim high. He said,

Paradise has one hundred levels and between each two levels is a distance like that between the Heavens and Earth. Al-Firdous is its highest level, from which four rivers of Paradise flow and above which is the Throne. When you ask from Allah, ask for Al-Firdaws.

Sunan Tirmidhi

We may not reach our aim, but by aiming high we will simply fall slightly lower.

My dear reader, aim for ihsaan. Aim to live each day aiming for Firdous al ala. Focus your intention wholeheartedly and know that you will find the manifestation of those deeds with big intentions waiting for you in the form of great reward in the afterlife.

Look around you and consider how you can practise ihsaan right now.

Right now, I am sitting alone in East London Mosque. It is 20.23pm. And the prayer hall has a total of four women. Two are talking, one is reading the Qur'an and I am sitting with my back against stone slabs that decorate the lower half of the hall. My legs are outstretched and my laptop is balancing on my knees. The contrast of my black socks against the emerald green carpet is rather striking. I can hear cars pass by. Other than that, there is silence with the exception of a melody of silent chatter and recitation.

I can practise ihsaan right now by praying two extra nawaafil salah. I do not have to. But I can purely for the sake of my Lord. I could stack the chairs into one neat pile, creating more space for future worshippers. I do not have to. But I could purely for the love of Allah. I could walk over to the two sisters, shake their hands, smile and give salaam (greeting). I could thank the sister who is reciting Qur'an and tell her how soothing it is to hear her voice as I type these words. I could walk over to the bathroom and neaten the sandals people use for the bathroom. Again, I do not have to – but doing these small simple deeds with the knowledge Allah is watching me as I do them: this is ihsaan. These simple actions are for Him and Him Alone.

Taqwa is the road to Allah. Ihsaan is you pausing on that road to pick up provisions to take with you to Him.

The beautiful relationship between ihsaan and taqwa is that both make you discover Allah in the ordinary, which become a means of being with Him in the Final Resting Place – which is so very extraordinary.

Worship Allah as though you see Him. Though you cannot see Him, He sees you.

Let Your Heart Ponder . . .

'Everyone goes back to Allah when they die, but happiest are those who go to Him while still alive.'

Syed Qutb

Du'a Invitation

Ar-Raqib, The All-Watcher, in every moment, remind me to ask myself this question: 'By placing You, My Lord at the centre of this, knowing You can see me, what should be my next move?'

Journal

1. Write down three things you do every day without fail.

....

....

2. What greater intentions can you set for these things? Write them down.

....

....

3. What act of worship does your heart incline towards?

....

....

4. How can you have ihsaan in this?

....

....

5. For the rest of today, focus your heart in being present. At every given opportunity, privately, do whatever you are doing with ihsaan.

....

....

**My reflections
on the topic of Ihsaan are . . .**

DAY 14

Self-love

My fingers are shaking as I write this. Before I begin in earnest, knowing the potential backlash this may cause, I wish to share something I wrote last year:

One of the greatest acts of courage is to share our truth, our story; to share all that we are. This is often perceived as being about having the courage to be vulnerable enough to share all of ourselves and our backstory with another person. But it is not. The spectators who witness this level of sharing are simply a means; an audience who will take what they wish, leave what they dislike and attach meaning in the way that they need to.

Sharing our truth and story is the greatest act of courage and vulnerability – not due to the spectators and witnesses involved. Rather, sharing is a means to giving ourselves permission to take centre stage to *see* ourselves perhaps for the first time in our lives. And *that* takes courage. That is true vulnerability.

Our lives are an intricate mix of joy, pain, failure, success, mistakes and triumphs. We select what we share with others – because we desire for others to see the best of us. We also pass through life, selecting what we allow ourselves to see of ourselves. To sit with ourselves and to be vulnerable enough to say 'This is me', is no easy task. And yet it is necessary – it is the only way to live authentically. It is what leads to happiness.

In only giving parts of ourselves to people, we are, unknowingly, only giving parts of ourselves to our own souls – therefore depriving ourselves of a true vulnerable experience with the most important person in our lives: our own self.

When I announced my divorce to the father of my four children, I knew there would be shock, disappointment, shame and blame. I received them all from the community. This is the cost of being in the public eye.

For others, my ex-husband and I were a golden couple. Him – a haafidh and Qur'an teacher (may Allah bless him) – and me – the founder and CEO of a charity. We were a couple who supported one another. We home-schooled our children and we chose to make hijrah. All aesthetic successes. So yes, it did come as a shock – particularly when I wrote a post that I had married a good man and divorced a good man. It did not make sense to the masses. They were of course not privy to the reasons why we did divorce.

Taking such a step was far from easy. It was not an overnight decision. And it was not born out of hate. It was hard – especially as I came from a divorced household where I had vowed never to divorce if I had children myself.

This may not make sense to you, my dear reader, nor does it need to. But that difficult decision was born from a place of self-love. I know, as with other things I have said and done, I will be labelled as a radical feminist, someone who is trying to destroy the institution of Islamic marriage, propagating divorce, causing issues within Muslim households and just being outright selfish. Yet I am simply a woman; a human being amongst billions who is sharing her story and her truth.

I believe in marriage. I also believe a successful marriage

takes time and great effort to make it work – especially after children and as the years go by. I believe firmly that one should try everything before even thinking about divorce.

I also believe my soul is more important than anything else. It is more important than a husband, my parents and my children. My soul before Allah comes first. And I believe this is true self-love.

My other belief is that self-love is an act of worship on this journey of taqwa. When I am looking after my soul – a creation of Allah – I am in fact worshipping Him. When my soul comes first, I remember the Creator of my soul. And when I remember the Creator, I pass through life as though I can see Him while knowing that I am under His Watchful Gaze.

Allah ('azza wa jal) tells us,

> Successful indeed is the one who purifies their soul, and doomed is the one who corrupts it!
>
> Surah Ash-Shams 91:9–10

For a very long time, I lived my life placing my soul at the bottom of the pile. I placed so many other people and their needs above it.
There is a hadith which states:

> Whoever is concerned about the Hereafter, Allah will place richness in his heart, bring his affairs together, and the world will inevitably come to him. Whoever is concerned about the world, Allah will place poverty between his eyes, disorder his affairs, and he will get nothing of the world but what is decreed for him.
>
> Sunan Tirmidhi

By prioritising my soul, I am concerned with my akhirah. Everything else is secondary and should be a means towards the akhirah and not the goal in this life.

When you love yourself and your soul intensely because your eyes are on Jannah, you are compelled to make certain choices, decisions and changes that prioritise your journey to Him.

That may mean small changes, or it may mean big changes. It may mean that you disappoint people and sometimes even hurt them. My divorce hurt others. That is very difficult for me to write. This was the cost of putting my soul first. I wish they had never been hurt. I wish things could have been different. But ultimately my soul – in its obedience to Allah and in protecting it from disobedience and striving to do that which I am not obligated to do to seek nearness to Him – took precedence. And I ask Allah to forgive me for any wrong therein.

Now, one might ask, 'What about the souls of your children, for whom you are responsible?' It is most certainly a valid question and one I asked myself for years. I then reminded myself that I am a mother who is responsible to teach them their deen, to encourage them towards good character and to live happy, fruitful lives on their own journeys to Him. In order for me to do that, my soul must receive the oxygen mask of faith before I can even think of placing oxygen masks on them.

Self-love, or rather soul-love, is crucial on this journey. If you do not love and prioritise your soul, which certainly will return to Allah, what are you in fact living and breathing for? People, things, fame, experiences – none of which you will take with you when you leave this world.

But by prioritising yourself, other people, things, fame and experiences become means for that future goal. You become a different son or daughter, husband or wife, friend, student, employee or employer. Your possessions become a means on the journey. You choose fame with Allah through your good deeds. You choose experiences that will move you towards Him or even experiences that provide you with joy, rest and rejuvenation to strengthen you so that you can continue on your journey of taqwa.

Self-love forces you to be present – because at every given

moment, you evaluate whether this person or thing is the best thing for yourself on this journey to Allah. You are constantly present asking yourself, 'Does this benefit my soul? Will this still benefit my soul?'

In this blessed month, as you go about your worship and evaluate yourself and your life, in preparation for asking Allah for all that your heart desires as you approach Laylatul Qadr, the extensive worship of the Night of Power when the Qur'an was revealed to the Prophet (ﷺ), immerse yourself in self-love. This is sadaqa jariah (charity that continues after death) for your soul – for when we love ourselves, the manifestation will reach the gates of Jannah – bi'idhnillah (by Allah's Permission).

The writer Andrea Dykstra puts it well when she says, 'In order to love who you are, you cannot hate the experiences that shaped you.' As I said, I was really nervous about writing about my divorce. But then I realised that vulnerability is self-love. Sharing your vulnerability with others is actually about over-coming fear in order to look at yourself deeply and honestly – and taking all of yourself in. Accepting and embracing all of your-self. And upon doing so, deciding whether you are going to move forward and live a life of being open and honest, embrac-ing vulnerability, or if you are going to turn back and continue to wear a mask not only in front of others, but also with yourself.

I give a little smile this morning because I choose the former. I choose to accept Aliyah and her story. I choose to commit to living a life where I embrace the unknown and take risks. I choose to follow this path of vulnerability that great individuals in history have taken before me. I choose to be myself fully and to manage courageously all that comes with doing so.

More than that, I smile because I kinda like the Aliyah I now see – all of her. It is as though I have been introduced to her for the first time. And through this, permission has been given for this author to begin to write one of the greatest love stories. It is finally time for this honest, open, courageous and vulnerable love affair with Aliyah to unravel and unfold.

Today, let us end with a hadith:

> Abdullah ibn Hisham reported: We were with the Messenger of Allah (ﷺ) and he was holding the hand of Umar ibn al-Khattab. Umar said to him, 'O Messenger of Allah, you are more beloved to me than everything but myself.' The Prophet said, 'No, by the one in whose hand is my soul, your faith is not complete until I am more beloved to you than yourself.' Umar said, 'Indeed, I swear by Allah that you are more beloved to me now than myself.' The Prophet (ﷺ) said, 'Now you are right, O Umar.'
>
> Bukhari

There are many lessons about self-love in this hadith.

Firstly, we find that Umar (may Allah be pleased with him) was vulnerable enough to declare his self-love in a public setting amongst the Prophet and his companions. Secondly, the Prophet (ﷺ) did not tell Umar he was wrong for loving himself. He (ﷺ) approved of Umar (may Allah be pleased with him) loving himself as he did not correct it. He (ﷺ) corrected that Umar's self-love should be secondary to his soul-love. Soul-love being a prioritisation of Allah and what and whom He loves. In doing so, we are truly loving ourselves because we prioritise that which is most beneficial for our soul's journey. Lastly, because Umar loved himself enough, he was immediately able to turn his heart towards loving the Prophet (ﷺ) more than himself, as the very act of doing this was an extension of his self-love.

Love yourself lavishly.
Your soul needs it.
Your soul deserves it.

Let Your Heart Ponder . . .

This time, choose your soul.

Du'a Invitation

I am pleased with Allah as a Lord, with Islam as a religion, and with Muhammad as a Prophet.

Journal

1. Is your soul a priority in your life?

....

....

....

....

2. What needs to change in order for it to become one?

....

....

....

....

3. How can you make Allah and His Messenger more beloved to you?

....

....

....

....

**My reflections
on the topic of Self-love are . . .**

DAY 15

Self-talk

When my eldest child was two years old, we began the journey of hifdh – memorising the Qur'an. In the early days it was fun and playful with stickers as rewards which grew into gifts for every surah or part of the Qur'an that she memorised. When she was very young, she would find longer surahs difficult to memorise. I remember her being around three years old, memorising Juz Tabarak (the twenty-ninth part of the Qur'an) and whining, 'It's too difficult. Ummi, I can't do it.'

I bent down so I was at her level and looked straight into her big brown eyes and told her, 'You are not allowed to say "I can't" again. You can say it is hard. You can say it is difficult. But never say "I can't". Because you can. And Allah will help you.'

To this day, now a young woman, she catches herself if she ever thinks 'I can't' and stops herself saying it, hearing my voice in her head. I have witnessed her go through the challenges of trying to achieve her goals – putting in more effort than most to prove that she can, because she knows it is possible.

Ramadan is a month of dialogue. It is a month of du'a, istighfaar and tawbah. We talk to Allah more in this month than any other time in the year. While we are paying attention to how we talk to Allah, I wish to point out the importance of paying attention to how we speak to ourselves. I believe this directly shapes the experiences we have with ourselves, others and Allah. Du'a is the manifestation of how much we love Allah. Self-talk is the manifestation of self-love.

The belief that 'we can' and that 'Allah can' is the type of training we need to offer ourselves. And I know that for us adults it is harder to make changes in how we speak to ourselves but it is most certainly not impossible. There are certain statements I unconsciously tell myself which I realise do not serve me at all, but they are so deeply rooted, they are thought and spoken internally without me realising. We all have these inner voices, which are actually external voices that we have internalised as our own. We need to silence these voices and say, 'No more.'

When I gave birth to my second child – the second of my children born by emergency C-section – I was told by the health visitor that if I ever wanted to have another child, it would most definitely be another C-section. I was told it would be impossible for me to have a natural delivery after two caesareans. After falling pregnant with my third child, I said, 'I can and Allah can' and joined VBAC groups and birthed him in water.

When I had the idea to set up a charity that supported female reverts in difficulty, I was told by close friends that it would be impossible for me to do – what with two children aged five and two and my youngest only six months old, and home-schooling. I said, 'I can and Allah can', and held the first-ever meeting in my living room as I rocked my six-month-old in his bouncer. The charity Solace UK launched three months later and, Alhamdulillah, has been serving revert sisters for the past twelve years.

When I was worried I would not find the time to write this book, I forced myself to say, 'I can and Allah can', knowing that nothing is impossible. The fact that you are holding this book is proof. All praise and thanks are due to Him Alone.

There are so many things we tell ourselves that do not serve our purpose. I am focusing on the phrase 'I can't' because this contaminates so many areas of our lives. It takes us away from being present and directly impacts our God-conscious journey. When we say 'I can't', we are saying it is not possible for us, nor is it possible for Allah to make it possible for us. This negatively changes our perception of Allah. It weakens our determination to reach Him and His Gardens of Delight. If we are constantly telling ourselves, 'I can't', then that becomes our focus and filters out to our belief that we can't with Allah and He 'can't' with us. We become people who see impossibility instead of possibility.

The days of our lives are full of moments where we can either tell ourselves we can or we can't. When we wake up in the morning, we can either tell ourselves, 'I can't get through today', or, 'It's possible for me to do the best I can today'. As we go about our day, we can tell ourselves, 'I can make the right decision by seeking Allah's Help', 'I can do this', 'I can choose my response to this', 'I can be present', and 'I can have ihsaan with this'. As we end our days, we can tell ourselves, 'Today was seriously tough and I can do better tomorrow for His Sake.'

'I can't' takes us away from the present moment. It is about saying I cannot do this because I failed in the past or because I am too afraid of failing in the future. Either way, we are not present. 'I can' automatically means that right now you believe you can and are able. So it instantly grounds you in the present – finding ways to prove you can here and now. If you want to be present, say 'I can' more. To help yourself do this, ask yourself two honest questions:

1. 'Is this possible for me?' The answer is always yes – even if it takes people, resources, time – there is nothing that makes it an absolute-inscribed-in-stone fact that it is impossible. It is just your mind that says it is.

2. 'Is it possible for Allah?' Knowing Allah's Power, Strength and Ability – that He is the Creator of the largest mammal swimming a vast ocean and the tiny ant scuttling the earth – do you think it is impossible for Him to make this possible for you?

So yes, you can!

It is this level of training that is required to produce self-talk that will add value to your two lives – this one and the next.

Now, in order to grasp the words and phrases you use, you will need to slow down. Our inner voice is often so fast with its chatter that we cannot catch up! It is by slowing down and being present that you will be able to hear the way your self-talk interferes with your relationship with yourself, others and Allah.

After slowing down, catch what you are saying and apply a very quick litmus test to it: 'Is this an absolute truth?' Challenging yourself in this way is you fighting your nafs (ego). It is the true meaning of striving.

The Prophet (ﷺ) said,

> There is no Muslim who plants a tree or sows seeds and then a bird, or a person, or an animal eats from it except that it is regarded as a charity for him.

> Bukhari

You are rewarded for the good treatment of animals who are not accountable before Allah. What then of the good treatment of yourself by speaking kindly, respectfully and with compassion to yourself – a being who is accountable? Subhan'Allah.

To be conscious of God is to be conscious of the self. When you are conscious of yourself, you are aware of what you feed your soul. How we perceive God and live with Him consciously is affected by how we perceive and live with ourselves. Please read that again.

Your self-talk can either place you in a position of presence and thus immerse you in being conscious of Allah, right now; or it can dump you in the landfills of the past and future, – taking you away from being conscious of Allah. Consciousness of Allah is a thing you do actively, in the present. Don't let your self-talk take you away from that.

Pay attention to what you say to yourself and about yourself.

Let Your Heart Ponder . . .

'Allah says, "I am as My servant thinks I am." Not only is Allah who you perceive Him to be, so too, you are and will become who you think yourself to be. Think well of yourself. Choose your thoughts wisely.'

Aliyah Umm Raiyaan

Du'a Invitation

Al-Khabir, The All-Aware, You are a Lord who loves Truth. You grant Your servants understanding. You guide them to become better and more insightful. Al-Aziz, The Almighty, I am weak. There is a battle in my mind. I sometimes suffer from my own thoughts. Negative thoughts attack me. They limit me. They create darkness in my life. They chain me and hold me back from moving towards You. My thoughts cause problems for me, my family and my desired journey to You. Allah, help me. Heal me. Silence the negative thoughts in my head. Let me speak and hear only that which will be of benefit to me in this life and the next. Fill my internal voice with words that are true, respectful, just towards myself, compassionate, moving and enabling. Al-Karim, You are so Generous. You are Al-Lateef – intervene between myself and my thoughts. You are Kinder than I am to myself. Help me to treat myself in semblance of how You treat me.

Journal

1. Name three recent things you want that you have told yourself you can't do or have. Challenge yourself – is it absolutely true that you can't?

....

....

....

2. Next to each of the above things, with Allah's attributes in mind, write down why Allah can make it possible for you.

....

....

....

3. My self-talk is interfering with my desire to be present and conscious of Allah in the following ways . . .

....

....

....

4. This is what I can do about it . . .

....

....

....

**My reflections
on the topic of Self-talk are . . .**

DAY 16

Uni-tasking

People often ask me, 'How do you do it? Run a charity, home-educate your children and all your household responsibilities – how do you manage it?'

The honest answer is, 'I struggle to do it all.'

I recently heard the American author Simon Sinek say, 'Every single good thing that happens in our lives comes at a cost. There's nothing free.' When I heard this, I wanted to write it out and frame it. It is so very true. The cost for me has been overwhelm.

For years, I have struggled with being overwhelmed. It has been the number one reason why my self-talk goes haywire! And I continue to struggle with being overwhelmed. I struggle because my load is literally so heavy sometimes that I feel unable to carry it all.

I know I have choice. I could put down my load. I accept I have chosen to continue to carry it. I choose to continue as I feel these things are far more important to me.

I remember reading another quote from an unknown author, who said,

Marriage is hard. Divorce is hard. Choose your hard.

Obesity is hard. Being fit is hard. Choose your hard.

Being in debt is hard. Being financially disciplined is hard. Choose your hard.

Communication is hard. Not communicating is hard. Choose your hard.

I have chosen my hard. But I have also chosen to find ways to make it easier. It has very much been a case of trial and error.

Initially I tried to find a better time-management system to fit it all within twenty-four hours. In fact, approaching my time with a 168-hours-per-week mindset did help! Thanks to the ideas of Stephen Covey, it developed into dealing with the big things first. Additionally, I tried to multi-task – with the view that by doing more than one thing at once, I would have time to do even more! And I kept experimenting with new methods to get more done.

It was all about the doing.

It was only when I was hit with a major difficulty in the year 2020 that led me to almost lose myself that I started therapy and learnt that my constant 'doing, doing, doing' was a way of avoiding the deeper stuff: seeing myself – my scars, my vulnerabilities and what needed healing. It did not matter that I had discovered a new system or time-management guru, I would constantly experience overwhelm because I had this drive to do, do, do.

I identified what was no longer a priority for me on this journey to Allah, and put it down. Other things that were of importance to me went through changes such as recruiting new staff at Solace UK, delegating to others and enlisting tutors to help home-school my children.

But the one thing that continues to make a difference – and which I have pledged to do more of, as much as I can – is to uni-task with as many things as possible.

Our purpose in life is not to be busy until we pass out. We are not required to fill every waking hour with something. Our purpose in life is to worship Allah with God-consciousness, sincerity, humility and presence.

This is where uni-tasking comes in. And it is not something

new. It is something the month of Ramadan teaches us. Suhoor (pre-dawn meal) has its time. Iftar has its time. Taraweeh (Ramadan prayer) has its time. Night prayer has its time. Even outside of Ramadan, each salah has its appointed time.

Uni-tasking is where you do one thing at a time with full effort, attention and most importantly presence. It means you make a conscious decision to devote yourself to the task at hand and immerse yourself in it completely.

When we think about uni-tasking, we normally think of it in terms of study or work. But uni-tasking is something that needs to be applied to everything – study, work, leisure, relationships and worship.

When my youngest child was little, she would often approach me with something amazing she wished to share. If I was busy with work, I would respond to her while simultaneously working. With her little hands, she would grab my face and turn it towards her, demanding my attention. She was very young at the time but this was her way of telling me that she needed my full attention.

Uni-tasking is not something I have mastered. I am sure if you were to ask my loved ones, they will tell you this is still very much a work in progress! It is something I am committed to practise and incorporate in my life; training myself until it insha'Allah (God willing) becomes my default position.

When I was a new Muslim, I would take my little book of Hisnul Muslim (a book of du'a to make in all situations) and make as much du'a as I could. Waking up, going to the market, getting dressed, entering the mosque, experiencing times of stress, visiting the sick, entering and exiting the bathroom – I was surprised there was a specific du'a to make for pretty much every situation a person might find themselves in. And I wish to return to that. Because over two decades later, I realise the existence of these situational du'a is a lesson in presence and an encouragement towards uni-tasking. The act of making du'a in these moments shows us that uni-tasking is the only way to truly immerse yourself in an experience, attribute it to Allah and find Him there.

Uni-tasking is incredibly important on this journey of taqwa. If research has shown that multi-tasking negatively affects performance and decreases productivity, can you imagine how multi-tasking is negatively affecting our mental health and relationships – including the most important of them all – with the Lord of the Worlds?

Uni-tasking means that your twenty minutes of reading the Qur'an is for that purpose only. No distractions, no picking up your phone and scrolling through social media in between. It means complete immersion in the words of Allah ('azza wa jal).

Uni-tasking means that when you are cooking, you really see the colours and feel the textures of the ingredients – taking in the amazing sights and smells as you prepare your meal.

Uni-tasking, when you tell a loved one you love them, means telling them you love them with your eyes, facial expressions and body language in unison with your words.

Uni-tasking is focusing completely on the act of giving sadaqa – the decision of how much, for whom and the giving of it – correcting your intention, maximising your intention and telling Allah ('azza wa jal) this is for Him, because you love Him.

Uni-tasking is essential on this journey of taqwa. Uni-tasking increases your chance of being conscious of Allah because by practising it as much as possible with things and people, you have trained yourself to be conscious of Him.

In the simple act of communicating, the Prophet (ﷺ) taught us the importance of uni-tasking. Abū Hurayrah (may Allah be pleased with him) reported that:

> When he turned (to you), he turned his whole body,
> and when he turned away, he would turn his whole
> body away.
>
> Musnad Aḥmad

Dear reader, I have a question for you. By consciously deciding to uni-task, what are you turning your complete self to face and how might that positively turn you towards your goal of nearness to Him ('azza wa jal)? And by not uni-tasking, what might you be missing?

I invite you to experience uni-tasking right now.

Choose something that you need to or want to do. Ask yourself if this is something you most definitely want to do or need to do right now. If yes, focus on the fact you have made the choice to do it. Hone in on the reasons why you want to do it. If the idea of doing something else comes to mind, place it on a shelf in your mind.

Now, make room physically so that all you are doing is the task at hand. That might mean telling loved ones that you will be unavailable for the next fifteen minutes. It might mean turning off notifications on your devices. It might be about making du'a for strength and help before you start. Now, give yourself fully to the task at hand. Be present physically, mentally, emotionally and spiritually.

If you have read this next line and have not done the above activity, pause. I recommend that you do it before reading on. Your life and your journey to taqwa depend very much on making changes in the present.

Regardless of how the experience felt, know that you will be required to practise this until it becomes your default position.

What I do know is it will mean more quality, less overwhelm and more happiness as you do what you love with the time, presence and attention it deserves. And guess what – have the intention that this is all for Allah and He will love what you are doing too.

Uni-tasking leads you to the One.

Let Your Heart Ponder . . .

'To do two things at once is to do neither.'

Publilius Syrus

Du'a Invitation

Ya Allah, assist me in focusing myself on all my experiences so that I may be present enough to enjoy them, benefit from them, benefit others with them and correct my intentions to make them for You.

Journal

1. Write down all the things you need to do tomorrow.

....

....

....

2. Rewrite your list by prioritising the most important at the top, down to the least important at the bottom.

....

....

....

3. Next to each activity write down all the distractions that need to be parked on the shelf.

....

....

....

4. Next to each activity write down how you can be fully immersed in it physically, mentally, emotionally and spiritually.

....

....

....

My reflections on
the topic of Uni-tasking are . . .

DAY 17

Life Audit

I n Ramadan 2010, I was making a du'a I often make: 'Oh Allah, use me for this deen.'

As I was a busy mother of three young children at the time, it used to be the simple little things that would bring me calm. One of them was my alone time in the shower. In fact, apart from sleep, it was the only time I could be alone with my thoughts.

One day, during Ramadan, while in the shower, my time for nothingness was blasted with thought after thought. It caught me by surprise. I began to think about my journey over the last eleven years as a revert to Islam. Flashback images came at me in quick succession. Sitting on the plush carpet of my friend's living room in a blue tie-dyed scarf, carefully declaring the foreign words of the declaration of faith. Buying metres of material to make myself an abaya (Islamic dress) from Whitechapel market. Bookshop basements where I attended Islamic lectures.

Painful images also hit me – my step-father who brainwashed my mother into telling me at the age of seventeen that her job as a mother was done and I was now on my own. Images of me lying in a hospital bed at the age of eighteen – alone. An image of the white door to my room in Hendon and the landlord banging on it demanding rent after I had lost my job. I saw an image of me placing all my hijabs, books and any other reminder of Islam in a box and putting it in the loft – after life had become too difficult as a new Muslim. The image brought tears to my eyes – I had almost lost the most precious thing to me: my faith. I had gone through so much in such a short space of time.

Then I kept remembering other fellow revert women who were struggling with their identity and their families – kicked out for becoming Muslim, married and divorced, single mothers, loneliness, depression – the lot.

Right there, in the middle of the shower, a fire rose inside me until it burnt fiercely. Something had to be done. Treating a new revert as a novelty had to stop. The difficulties a new Muslim encounters, and the impact such a transition can have, require support.

And at that thought, I felt this sudden responsibility – that I had to do something. I could see images of future new Muslims, and knew that it could not go on like this. In a very short space of time, my thoughts turned to developing a support system: an organisation that would offer a female Muslim revert in difficulty all that she would need to thrive with her newly found faith. The vision was clear. I could see all the ways this could become possible.

I rushed out of the shower, grabbed a piece of paper and a pen and began brainstorming this idea. There were lines and circles, smudged by droplets of water. I could not stop. I was scared to stop. I did not want to miss a thing. Once I had finished, there was a feeling inside me that is still present to this day: I had found my personal mission.

Three months later, Solace UK was born.

Today, Solace UK is a registered charity that provides various types of post-Shahaadah support for women who have reverted to Islam. Solace UK is my fifth child, my baby. I find it difficult to switch off from Solace UK, just like a mother cannot switch off from her child.

I love what I do because I have personally been there and want to do everything in my power to prevent fellow revert women from going through what I did. But while I love my job as CEO of Solace UK and work with a fantastic team of like-minded women, there are parts of the job that I cannot stand. One of them is the annual independent examination of our accounts. Maths is not my thing at all and the responsibility of ensuring that every penny of charity money has been spent wisely really weighs heavily on me. Though I dread looking at Excel sheets as I review the accountant's work on our annual accounts, though my toes curl when the independent examiner comes back with his long list of specific questions about this transaction or this decision, I know it is all necessary – not only for the amanah (upholding of trust) in how we have spent funds but also because it is a good reflection for myself and the other trustees to see how we fared over the past year and what changes need to be made to be and do better.

I think you know where I am going with this. We need to do a regular audit of our lives. We must. Umar bin al-Khattab advised, 'Call yourselves to account before you are called to account.' Every second, minute, hour, day, week, month and year that passes – we are moving closer to death. This is a fact. We live so much in the abstract realm but struggle with the facts of reality. Every day we are getting older and moving closer to the final destination. And as I have previously said, the next stop on the journey to that destination may be closer than we realise.

Time is precious. Life is precious.

I started this book with an invitation to pause and reflect. And now, on Day 17 of Ramadan, before we enter the last ten nights with our du'a lists and everything that we want to ask Allah for the coming year, it is time to do an audit.

It is time to sit with who you are, where you are currently at and do a thorough check of your life.

Let's do an audit right now!

Let Your Heart Ponder . . .

Decide what kind of dunya and akhirah you really want. And then say no to everything that is not that.

Du'a Invitation

Al-Aleem, The All-Knowing, I ask you by Your Knowledge of all that You Know of my past, my present and future to guide me to make the best choices for my soul. Direct my thoughts and heart to decisions that will benefit me in all areas of my life. Give me the strength to let go of that which is of no benefit. Show me what needs to change. Bring me all that I need to steer me in the best direction in all of my affairs.

O Ever Living, O Self-Subsisting and Supporter of all, by Your Mercy I seek assistance, rectify for me all of my affairs and do not leave me to myself, even for the blink of an eye.

Journal

1. Say Bismillah ('In the name of Allah'). Focus on the meaning of the Bismillah.

....

....

....

2. In this or another journal, or on a separate piece of paper, write down the following – one for each page:

- My relationship with Allah

- Myself (physical, mental and emotional wellbeing)

- My family (parents, spouse, siblings, extended family)

- Work/Study

- Wealth

- Friends

- Social life/Leisure

3. For each of the above categories, answer the following questions:

- What is going well?

- How can I use what is going well to aid me in my journey to Allah and His Akhirah?

- What isn't going well?

- What can I change to positively impact my relationship with Allah?

- How present am I in these areas?

- How can I become more present in these areas?

- What do I need to say 'Yes' to?

- What do I need to say 'No' to?

- If I made all of the above changes, my life on this journey to Allah would become . . .

**My reflections on
the topic of a Life Audit are . . .**

DAY 18

Acceptance

This book has been written in coffee shops, the mosque, in the seating area as my youngest attended a swimming class, and in the car. I carry my laptop everywhere with me – sometimes because I literally need to fit in the writing wherever and whenever I can to free up some time. Occasionally, I need to take myself away from my normal home environment and be somewhere quiet where the silence allows me to reflect and write.

Last night, after serving up dinner, I left home and found a café not far from East London Mosque that was open until late. I sat down, opened my laptop, surrounded by silence, and thought yes, I can write a chapter today. I was ready to write. But I was blank. Completely blank. No words came. I began to force words out in an attempt to make the most of this precious time alone to meet my quota of writing a chapter a day. But the words just would not come. Here I was writing a chapter about the importance of acceptance in the pursuit of being present and I had a serious case of writer's block.

After nearly an hour of being frozen and a blank page with the exception of 'Day 18 – Acceptance' at the top, I shut my laptop, stuffed it into my tote bag and walked defeated back to my car. In the five-minute journey back home, I kept repeating 'La hawla wa la quwwata illa billah' (There is no Might or Power except with Allah), remembering hearing that it opens doors. I was desperate for the door of my mind to open so that words could pour forth! When I arrived home, I attempted to force out some thoughts – but writer's block still reigned supreme.

And then a thought occurred to me: I need to accept that I am stuck. There is no use in trying to force out words as they will not come from my heart. I want my words to come from deep within me. So I gave in and went to bed. While lying in bed, in between sleep and wakefulness, it came to me – this is how you need to start this chapter. Presence can never be a fabrication of what we feel we should do or how we feel we should be. Presence is an acceptance of who we are and where we are right now.

As I drifted off to sleep, I knew tomorrow I had to start exactly there: a writer who was completely frustrated and blocked – knowing where I want to go but completely at a standstill as to how to get there.

We know we have a job to do: to worship Allah with as much presence as possible, and to do everything we can to earn His Pleasure. Sometimes we will know what steps to take. Yet weighing up whether we are on track, as we did in yesterday's chapter, may leave us feeling lost, confused and stuck.

When we feel this way, we feel we can only show up to Allah when the block is removed, when the confusion clears and once we know what to do next. But you see, Allah loves the humble needy soul. We can show up to Allah in all our seasons. We show up when we know and when we do not know. We show up when life is flowing and when life feels like it has come to a halt. We show up by accepting where we are right now is where we need to be right now. We show up by being present with the blocks of our heart and in our life. We do that by accepting this is how we feel right now, feeling all of the emotions and allowing them to pass when they need to. These blocks on our journey are necessary. They do not prevent us from moving closer to Allah. They are like roadblocks on a journey where we need to present our identity documents to Allah and say, 'Here I am. This is all of me. I need Your help to pass onto the next part of my journey.'

I am actually in tears as I write this because the very block that I experienced last night has made me revisit everything I have written thus far and change it. The chapters you have read so far were rewritten after this very moment. I identified that the block was caused by trying to fit the chapters into a structure suggested by my editor. I emailed her to say that this did not feel right and I needed to write it in my own way. Her response was that she trusts me completely, which gave me room to change the previous seventeen chapters and write the rest of the book as me, in my own way.

See, this is what acceptance does. It allows for you to be who you are in every given moment. There is no mould you need to try to squeeze yourself into. There is no one universal formula. There is no script you need to adopt. It is just you, as your vulnerable honest self – coming to Allah both in flow and in block.

Presence is found in accepting the moments of your life. It is in accepting your emotions and states and offering them validation.

There is a beautiful poem by Rumi called 'The Guest House' that says,

> The human body in this world
> is like a guesthouse.
>
> Every morning a new arrival of
> depression, meanness or happiness
> comes as an unexpected visitor.
>
> You should be welcoming them all.
> And do remember that in this life,
> you are not held by the neck.

Still, treat each guest honourably.
For He may be clearing you out,
as a lesson.

Be grateful for whoever comes,
because each has been sent
as a guide from God.

Acceptance is to see your circumstances, experiences, feelings and states as messengers – with a Divine message to pass onto you.

How does this translate to the journey of God-consciousness? Well, when you are in flow, you acknowledge this is from Allah and you thank Him. When you are happy, you praise Allah for what you are feeling. When you are hurting, you run to Allah for Help. When your ego wants to take lead, you complain to Allah that it is hard to restrain yourself and beg Him to humble you. And when you are stuck, you accept that you are stuck and show up to Him with patience, for however long it takes until you are permitted to pass through.

This journey of taqwa is coming to Allah broken and stuck. We do not need to wait until we are healed and unstuck. This is the true journey of God-consciousness – to accept in the present moment all of our conditions and come to Him in all our seasons.

I end with a reflection I wrote a number of years ago:

Life is not greener on the other side.

Nor is life necessarily greener where you water it.

Life is greener wherever Allah, The Creator, nourishes and places His Barakah therein.

To busy oneself with the pursuit of finding that 'something else', and what we perceive is that 'something better' will not necessarily bring about something greener.

To busy oneself with the pursuit of seeking His Guidance, His Blessings and His Direction brings not only that which is greener but a colour to life that you never knew existed.

Accept yourself and your current state. Present yourself to Him.

Let Your Heart Ponder . . .

'Once we accept our limits, we go beyond them.'

Albert Einstein

Du'a Invitation

Al-Mumin, The Giver of Security, I need Your Assistance to help me with acceptance. I struggle to accept change. I struggle when I feel stuck. You know I yearn to be near You. You know the callings of my heart. I am in need of Your Help. Al-Lateef, The Most Subtle, The Kind, help me feel through my fears. Help me face my frustrations. You are a Lord that sees me for who I am and accepts me as I am. Help me live presently by accepting that all of my moments are my best moments even if I cannot see it at the time. Guide me as I choose to live a more present, God-centred life. Bless me with the courage to face the roadblocks of my life and to know they are simply resting points to present myself to You humbly and vulnerably.

Journal

1. What do you need to accept about yourself?

....

....

2. Go ahead and accept this is who you are right now. How do you feel?

....

....

3. What do you need to accept about your life right now?

....

....

4. Go ahead and accept this is where you're at right now. How do you feel?

....

....

5. Acceptance of who I am and where I am at right now becomes a catalyst for change in the following ways . . .

....

....

**My reflections on
the topic of Acceptance are . . .**

DAY 19

In Difficulty

My eldest daughter and I recently made a trip to visit Cambridge University. I had made all the preparations. Dropped my youngest daughter off at a friend's house. Sent any home-schooling class links ahead of time. Left my son with a schedule. Ensured there was food for lunch. Checked the route, made sure I had enough petrol and left ahead of time to ensure we would get there as soon as the open day began.

With everything taken care of, we left. The sky was blue and the sun was shining. It felt like one of the last warm days before the chill of autumn took over duty.

Joining the M11, I could see that it was going to take us less than an hour to get there. As we chatted away, me trying to use this golden opportunity to enjoy some one-to-one time with my eldest, consciously choosing to be present in our conversation, we heard a rumbling sound. I thought to myself, 'That's odd – the road feels really bumpy.' It became bumpier and bumpier and the sound became louder. I felt like I was losing control of the car. I immediately put my hazard lights on and pulled over onto the hard shoulder. I could smell burning rubber. Checking it was safe, I got out of the car and lo and behold the back tyre on the left-hand side had literally exploded.

It was just after 8.30am. I looked at my daughter and said, 'QadrAllah – maybe Allah has protected us from something far worse along the way or delayed things for us for a better reason.' On the hard shoulder, I made calls to emergency

166

breakdown companies. This in itself took more than an hour. After going through my insurance and booking a recovery service, we began the expected ninety minutes' wait. Looking at her long list of Cambridge colleges to visit, my daughter made du'a for it to be quicker. In fifteen minutes the recovery truck arrived. I wasn't shocked. Neither was she. We knew this was from Allah.

The gentleman in the truck took us to the nearest Kwik Fit which was fully booked. We were told it could take up to seven hours to fit us in. My daughter and I began to consider alternative transport. It was tempting to take one of these options but instead I said, 'Let's make du'a and wait.' So, after making du'a, we walked to the nearest Tesco to get some food. On the way back, we bumped into the Kwik Fit mechanic, who had finished repairing our car. It was 12.30pm.

It was nearly 2pm when we finally arrived in Cambridge. With hardly any time left, we had to whittle down our choices from visiting ten Cambridge colleges to only three – one of which my daughter was not fond of at all, choosing only to visit it because I asked her to. However, the visit was successful and interestingly my daughter ended up loving the very college she had previously said no to. I loved it too but had my reservations and took my concerns to Allah in du'a.

Two days later, as I sat in the prayer hall of East London Mosque, the wisdom of the car breakdown and delay became clear.

Life is like this. Sometimes you make all the necessary preparations to journey smoothly to your destination. You are present, motivated and ready to go. And then Allah sends something unexpected – something sudden – a challenge, a test, a difficulty that completely disrupts your plans. For a while, you cannot even think about journeying – you are focused on surviving. And that's okay.

Taqwa, presence and ihsaan are not linear. They are not smooth sailing. They are means along the journey where our imperfect selves travel to the Perfect One. So when you have been enjoying a smooth journey and then find yourself facing a huge mountain obstructing your path, forcing you to disrupt your journey and deal instead with how you are going to climb that mountain, know that this too is part and parcel of the journey.

In yesterday's chapter we looked at accepting that. Today, dear reader, allow me to speak to your heart.

When you are hit with a test, just as you attempt to rationalise it and force your heart to accept that this was written, you are hit with another. Then another. And another. Your soul is battered and bruised; you feel dazed – as though this is a nightmare that surely you will wake up from. You wonder how you can be served with not just one difficulty, but several all at once. You feel like your fragile heart cannot manage this. Where you could once see the image of your future before you, it is now obstructed by a mountain rooted firmly in the earth; a mountain you know you must climb in order to move forward into your future, into your life.

You do not know if your heart is racing or if it has slowed down to such an extent that it will collapse. So much confusion all around you and inside of you. All you can see is the distance from where you are now to the peak of the mountain, which signifies the halfway point. You wonder how on earth you are going to get there, knowing the descent will be much easier. Eyes fixed on the peak, you feel defeated and too tired to even contemplate the climb.

Pause. Stop. Breathe.

Remove your sight from the mountain, from the peak. The climb will occur at some point. It has to. It is a part of your reality. It is inevitable. But right now, there is something else that needs your attention. Something far more important.

It is time for preparation. Look around you.

Who will make the climb more difficult for you? Let them go for now.

Who will offer you support during the climb? Who will climb with you? Solicit their help.

Plan a schedule during which you will train your mind, body, heart and soul for the challenge ahead; days when you will simply rest to regather energy; and days when you will give it your all.

Break the challenge down into parts: on day one, I will attempt this part; on day two, that part. This part will be easier; this part will be more difficult. This part will require du'a the night before – in the last part of the night. This part will require me to let go of perfectionism and call on my tribe to climb with me.

Allah placed the mountain before you because He wants to stretch your climbing abilities. He wants to push you to your limits and only a mountain can do that. He wants you to face yourself in the mirror and acknowledge everything that is so very real about you – your strengths and your weaknesses. He wants you to see the tools he has scattered around you. Scattered, because He wants you to take the steps to reach out, collect them and use them. Then He will run to be your aid. Tools such as people who will literally stand behind you, ready to catch you as you climb; memories of previously climbed mountains – what you did then and what you can do now; memories of times where, despite being exhausted, you raised your hands towards the sky and begged Him for help, and He did. He wants to extract a stronger you from you. He wants a needier heart from you. He wants a soul that has accepted the challenge, persevered through it and emerged from the other side with lessons like no other.

You, who have a mountain in front of you, remember you are the same person who climbed your mountains of yesterday. Yesterday was brought to you by the same Lord that has brought you today and will bring your tomorrow. The mountains you climbed yesterday included the Best Guide – the Creator of the mountain. What does this mean? It means you have done this before with Him. You can do this again with Him. Different mountain, yes. But a stronger you with experience. A stronger heart who has already received guidance from the Ultimate Guide who knows you and this mountain inside and out.

Mountains are not sent just for the mere climb. They are sent to teach you so much about yourself and the One who made them and placed them before you. Gather your tools. Let go of anything that will weigh you down. Plan, train, rest, climb. Repeat.

You've got this. He has you. Let the ascent begin.

To return to the story at the start of this chapter, two days later I was sitting in the prayer hall of East London Mosque, having decided at the last minute not to go to a coffee shop. I prayed and sat down to write. There were two young women in their twenties in the opposite corner. We spent at least forty-five minutes sitting in silence until the adhaan of maghrib came – the call to sunset prayer.

After salah, one of the young women approached me and asked, 'Are you the sister from the YouTube channel *Honest Tea Talk?*'

Embarrassed, I replied, 'Yes.'

She explained how much she loved the show and asked whether I did university talks, to which I replied in the affirmative. Excited, she asked me if she could invite me to her ISOC (Islamic Society), to which I agreed.

'Oh, but it isn't in London,' she said with a worried look.

'Where is it?' I asked.

'Cambridge.'

I could not believe what I was hearing. 'I was there two days ago!' I exclaimed. I told her about the visit with my daughter, and she informed me she was a Cambridge student and part of the ISOC. She explained what a support the ISOC was for Muslim students at Cambridge. She then told me that it was the very college that my daughter had initially rejected – the one I had hoped she would at least consider and the one she fell in love with – that had the strongest Muslim sisterhood.

I immediately had goosebumps. The concerns that I had lifted up to Allah were being addressed through the words of this young sister in faith.

I knew then that the car breakdown had diverted us from the other colleges, forcing us due to time constraints to whittle down the list, so that my preference became her favourite choice too; and that Allah had wrapped it all up by placing comfort in my heart through directing me away from writing in a coffee shop to writing in the same room in East London Mosque as this young woman.

I remembered the words of the Prophet (ﷺ):

> Three supplications are answered and there is no doubt
> they will be answered: the supplication of the
> oppressed, the supplication of the traveller, and the
> parent for his child.
>
> Sunan Tirmidhi

My Lord's promise is always true.

Dear reader, you have chosen to heal from your past. You have chosen to become more present. When you are faced with a difficulty and you are unwillingly diverted from your smooth path – know that it may be an answer to your own du'a. You will come out of it more certain, stronger, and firmer in your belief of trust in Him.

For those who are struggling, I leave you with something I wrote during one of my lowest moments. May it bring you comfort as you continue, through your difficulty, on your journey to Him:

> To you who struggled to get out of bed this morning as
> you have done for the past few months. To you who
> finds yourself at the end of each day feeling empty. To

you who feels so confused as to why you feel so down. To you who struggles to do the basics. To you who is battling an 'invisible' illness but has to put on a brave face for the sake of the kids, spouse, family or in-laws. To you who feels guilty for feeling so down. To you who has struggled like this for years and doesn't know why. To you who tries your best to increase the practice of your faith and can't shake off feeling so very low. To you who doesn't know what to do or who to turn to. To you who feels ashamed for believing in Allah and wanting to end it all.

This message is for you.

What you are enduring is hard, tough, dark, lonely and unrelenting. It is there when you sleep and it is there when you wake up. It is there when you are around people and it is there when you are alone. It is confusing to others and even more confusing to yourself. It is debilitating and it feels like it will accompany you to the grave. You feel like no one understands and you are right – no one ever will, unless they have been there themselves. You have tried and you are tired of trying.

I want you to do just one thing. I want you to gather that atom's weight of will and energy you have left and do something right now. Not later. Not when there is a better time when you feel that little bit stronger. Right now. Regardless of what you were thinking or doing moments before. Do this right now.

I want you to turn to Allah and tell Him exactly how you feel. Tell Him that you feel you cannot do it anymore. Tell Him that you cannot cope. Tell Him the days are too hard. Tell Him the only reprieve is when you sleep. Tell Him that you need a break from this. Tell Him that you do not know what to do. Tell Him that you cannot do this on your own. Tell Him that you feel so alone. Tell Him exactly how this is crushing your mind, heart and soul.

Now I want you to acknowledge Him. I want you to feel in the depths of your chest that He is looking at you and hearing you at this exact precise moment. And this is exactly what is happening. He is looking at you right now, as you read this. He knows the patterns of your beating heart as you read this message. He is looking at you with such attention and intensity.

I want you to now believe with all of your heart that His Promise is going to reach you; His Promise that every du'a – your du'a – will be answered.

While acknowledging the Lord of the Universe looking at you and hearing you with such Love and Mercy, while holding onto the absolute truth that, in ways that are known to Him, your du'a will be answered, in your own way ask Him . . .

Allah, help me. My Lord, bring me absolutely everything that You know I need, so I may heal.

And He will. Believe He will. Internalise He will. For He says, I am as My servant thinks I am. He will because there is no heart that calls upon Him with such need and dependency, while enduring such difficulty, except that it is responded to in ways that demonstrate a Love and Precision that can only be from the Creator, the Beloved.

Do it right now and prepare yourself for the paths that emerge, the people He sends your way and the means to your relief and ease.

When you come across mountains . . .

Let Your Heart Ponder . . .

'It was from His Mercy that He blemished their worldly life for them and made it imperfect. This was so they would not feel comfortable in it nor feel secure regarding it, and so they would aspire for the endless enjoyment in His abode and in His company. So in reality, He deprived them so that He could give them, and He tried them so that He would relieve them, and He put them to death so that He would give them (everlasting) life.'

Ibn al-Qayyim, *Ighathat al-Lahfan*

'Tears are like messengers. They have the important messages of what's going on at the deepest part of your soul. They are telling you something so profound. Take heed of what they are saying. They are healing you for what lies ahead in your future.'

Aliyah Umm Raiyaan

Du'a Invitation

O Allah, I feel tired. This is so heavy for me. I am weak and I feel like I can't anymore. I hand it over to you completely. I submit to what You know will happen. Remind me, my Lord, of times where you stood by me as I fought battles and weathered storms. Remind me of my scars that You healed. Guide me to find strength in You. Let my eyes see the wisdom in all of this. I have, with Your help, climbed mountains before. I can do this, but only with You. Never let me forget that. Envelop me in Your Mercy. Carry me through this, ya Rabbi. I hand it over to You.

Journal

1. With the help of Allah, I have conquered the following mountains . . .

. . . .

. . . .

2. I conquered these mountains by . . .

. . . .

. . . .

3. Allah helped me by . . .

. . . .

. . . .

4. How can you conquer your current mountain – however big or small it is?

. . . .

. . . .

5. How might this mountain be a means of strengthening you for your ongoing journey to Allah?

. . . .

. . . .

**My reflections
on the topic of being
In Difficulty are . . .**

DAY 20

Allah, I Need to Talk to You about My Present

was in one of my favourite cafés in Hackney, East London. The table next to me was occupied by two Muslim women who resembled one another, with one looking like an older version of the other. I assumed they were mother and daughter. I love observing people and try to do so without them thinking I am a crazy woman invading their privacy!

It warmed my heart to see this mother and daughter duo seated at the table about to order a nice halal breakfast with one another. I pictured how pleased Allah was with the daughter who was honouring her mother with her time and company – knowing the reward given to the one who honours their parents and treats them with immense kindness.

As I sat there, glancing at them from time to time, I noticed something that changed my feelings to disappointment. After their food arrived, the daughter remained glued to her phone while her mother sat in silence as she ate. I observed the mother – where she sat up right when she initially walked in, her shoulders were now slumped, back bent as she slowly picked at her food. Her daughter's thumbs moved rapidly for the duration of their time there. She only looked up when she asked for the bill.

Immediately, I reminded myself not to judge. There could be a number of reasons why the daughter was absent instead of present. Perhaps there was a family emergency, or maybe there was a rift between the mother and daughter and just being in each other's presence was the first step towards rebuilding their relationship. There could be many reasons behind what I observed.

I left the truth of the situation to the only One who knew. But it did make me look at myself. As someone who is always incredibly busy and spends a lot of time on her phone, I reflected about the times my own loved ones may have been deprived of my presence and the impact that may have had on them and my relationship with them.

I left that café never wanting my loved ones to sit and look like that mother did. Knowing I was imperfect and that the journey towards being more present will always be a work in progress, I spoke to Allah and said, 'Help me.'

These last ten days of the second third of Ramadan, we have been working to become more present with ourselves, our loved ones and our Rabb.

It is time to talk to Allah.

Allah,

All glory is to You for all that You have created. All praise is for You for all that fills the earth and the sky. All thanks are to You for all the beauty of what we, Your creation, perceive through our senses. Through Your creation, I am provided with a glimpse of Your Beauty and Perfection. Thank You, Allah for allowing my senses to bask in the wonders of Your creation, providing me with a calming tranquillity in this life of distraction.

My Lord, have mercy upon Muhammad (ﷺ) and send peace upon him.

Oh my Beloved Lord, today is all I have. It is only Your Knowledge that knows whether I will see tomorrow. There are millions of graves full of people who said they would change tomorrow. Grant me the ability to treat each of my days as my last and change today. Take me upon the best of my deeds, with the purest state of heart and a soul that has been forgiven.

I wish to be most beloved to You. Guide my mind, heart and limbs to worship You as though I see You. Fill my mind and heart with a certainty that never dies, that You are constantly Watching me. Gift me with the honour of leaving this world as a muhsin.

Allah, there is so much I need to change to make the most of my present moments. Al-Wadood, You are the Most Loving, develop intense love for returning my soul back to You in its most sincere and humble state. Fill me with self-love so that I am always concerned with my soul and its connection with You.

Assist me in extending that soul-love to the way I speak to myself so that I may encourage and motivate myself to love and worship You.

Forgive me, Al-Ghafoor, this life distracts me constantly. When I forget, remind me. When I lose my way, bring me back to You. Grant me the ability to be present in my worship so that I worship not because I have to but out of love and yearning – because I want to.

With this concern for my soul's journey to You, Al-Mubeen, make it clear to me what needs to change, what needs to leave my life and what I need to bring into it. Ya Allah, remind me to take myself to account before I am taken to account.

And when I don't know how to do that, when I feel lost and stuck – I accept that this is when I need to turn to You more honestly, more needy – presenting myself in a vulnerable way like never before.

Allah, I yearn for You to be most pleased with me. My journey towards You will be bumpy. I acknowledge and accept that. I know that when it is, it is to teach me things about myself and draw out strengths that You know I will need for the rest of this journey. Just help me, please. When those bumps send me over the edge, catch me. I know You will. I trust You will.

As I continue to breathe, live and experience the present moments in my life, gift me with a deep consciousness to attribute and attach them all to You.

You are my Lord. I am Your humble slave. I devote myself to You.

Go back to the reflections on the topics
that you journaled about at the end of the
previous nine chapters. Read over them. Now
pen your own private thoughts about your present
to the One who is always present with you and for you.

PART 3:

Planning and Moving into an Akhirah-focused Future

'The Messenger of Allah (ﷺ) said: "What is the example of this worldly life in comparison to the Hereafter other than one of you dipping his finger in the sea? Let him see what he brings forth."'

Muslim

Write the chapters of your future so that the last chapter of your story ends beautifully.

Dear reader, I invite you to look ahead towards your akhirah-focused future.

DAY 21

The End

Come on a journey with me . . .
I extend an invitation to read each of the following sentences from the amazing and beautiful book *Haadi al-Arwaah ilaa Bilaad il-Afraah* by Ibn al-Qayyim with as much presence as possible, pausing between each one. With each pause, close your eyes and imagine your senses experiencing that which you have read.

Bismillah.

And if you ask about its ground and its soil, then it is of musk and saffron.

And if you ask about its roof, then it is the Throne of the Most Merciful.

And if you ask about its rocks, then they are pearls and jewels.

And if you ask about its buildings, then they are made of bricks of gold and silver.

And if you ask about its trees, then it does not contain a single tree except that its trunk is made of gold and silver.

And if you ask about its fruits, then they are softer than butter and sweeter than honey.

And if you ask about its leaves, then they are softer than the softest cloth.

And if you ask about its rivers, then there are rivers of milk whose taste does not change, and rivers of wine that is delicious to those who drink it, and rivers of honey that is pure, and rivers of water that is fresh.

And if you ask about their food, then it is fruits from whatever they will choose, and the meat of whatever birds they desire.

And if you ask about their drink, then it is Tasneem, ginger and Kaafoor.

And if you ask about their drinking cups, then they are crystal clear and made of gold and silver.

And if you ask about its shade, then a fast rider would ride in the shade of one of its trees for a hundred years and not escape it.

And if you ask about its vastness, then the lowest of its people would have within His Kingdom and walls and palaces and gardens the distance that would be travelled in a thousand years.

And if you ask about its tents and encampments, then one tent is like a concealed pearl that is sixty miles long.

And if you ask about its towers, then they are rooms above rooms in buildings that have rivers running underneath them.

And if you ask about how far it reaches into the sky, then look at the shining star that is visible, as well as those that are far in the heavens that the eyesight cannot possibly reach.

And if you ask about the clothing of its inhabitants, then they are of silk and gold.

And if you ask about its beds, then its blankets are of the finest silk laid out in the highest of its levels.

And if you ask about the faces of its inhabitants and their beauty, then they are like the image of the Moon.

And if you ask about their age, then they are young ones of thirty-three years in the image of Adam, the father of humanity.

Dear reader, how beautiful are these descriptions of Paradise. If this is not enough, Ibn al-Qayyim continues and describes a most beautiful day . . .

And if you ask about the Day of Increase (in reward) and the visit of the all-Mighty, all-Wise, and the sight of His Face – free from any resemblance or likeness to anything – as you see the Sun in the middle of the day and the full Moon on a cloudless night, then listen on the day that the caller will call: *'O People of Paradise! Your Lord – Blessed and Exalted – requests you to visit Him, so come to visit Him!'* So they will say: *'We hear and obey!'*

Until, when they finally reach the wide valley where they will all meet – and none of them will turn down the request of the caller – the Lord, Blessed and Exalted, will order His Chair to be brought there. Then, pulpits of light will emerge, as well as pulpits of pearls, gemstone, gold and silver. The lowest of them in rank will sit on sheets of musk, and will not see what those who are on the chairs above them are given. When they are comfortable where they are sitting and are secure in their places, and the caller calls: *'O People of Paradise! You have an appointment with Allah in which He wishes to reward you!'* So they will say: 'And what is that reward? Has He not already made our faces bright, made our scales heavy, entered us into Paradise, and pushed us away from the Fire?'

And when they are like that, all of a sudden a light shines that encompasses all of Paradise. So, they raise their heads, and, behold: the Compeller – Exalted is He, and Holy are His Names – has come to them from above them and honoured them and said: *'O People of Paradise! Peace be upon you!'* So, this greeting will not be responded to with anything better than: 'O Allah! You are Peace, and from You is Peace! Blessed are You, O possessor of Majesty and Honour!' So the Lord – Blessed and Exalted – will laugh to them and say: *'O People of Paradise! Where are those who used to obey Me without having ever seen Me? This is the Day of Increase!'*

So, they will all give the same response: 'We are pleased, so be pleased with us!' So, He will say: *'O People of Paradise! If I were not pleased with you, I would not have made you inhabitants of My Paradise! So, ask of Me!'* So, they will all give the same response: 'Show us Your Face so that we may look at it!' So, the Lord – Mighty and Majestic – will remove His covering and will honour them and will cover them with His Light, which, if Allah – the Exalted – had not Willed not to burn them, would have burnt them.

And there will not remain a single person in this gathering except that his Lord – the Exalted – will speak to him and say: *'Do you remember the day that you did this and that?'* and He will remind him of some of his bad deeds in the Worldly life, so he will say: 'O Lord! Will You not forgive me?' So, He will say: *'Of course! You have not reached this position of yours (in Paradise) except by My forgiveness.'*

So, how sweet is this speech to the ears, and how cooled are the righteous eyes by the glance at His Noble Face in the Afterlife . . .

Some faces that Day will be shining and radiant, looking at their Lord (Al-Qiyaamah:22–3)

Ibn al-Qayyim, *Haadi al-Arwaah ilaa Bilaad il-Afraah*

We get caught up with this dunya. We become so attached to it, as though we will live here for ever. We are on a temporary journey to our Permanent Home. Subhana'Allah – imagine not only entering upon Your Permanent Home, but also meeting the One who got you there.

When I find myself troubled within, confused or lost, this is often because my attachment to the akhirah is weak. This is very normal. Let us be real. We are working towards a place we have never seen. We are worshipping a Lord whose creation we see every day, but whom we cannot see. It is very normal to become attached to that which is tangible over that which is intangible.

Your commitment to your future in this dunya as well as your future of the akhirah lies in your faith. Not in simply having faith, as I was once told by the pastor of my church when I was a Christian, when I questioned him as to how a human being that ate and relieved himself could be the son of the Creator. But by renewing one's faith regularly and consistently.

When people ask me why I became Muslim, I tell them because I became rationally convinced that Islam was the truth. There was no way I would change my entire life based on an emotion that is fleeting. I embraced Islam because of the linguistic miracle of the Qur'an: the challenge Allah presented to humankind within the Qur'an itself to produce just a single verse like it in its level of grammar, eloquence and beauty – a challenge which, over 1400 years later has still not been met today. I embraced Islam because of the scientific miracles found within the pages of the Qur'an which were only confirmed later by science with the invention of the microscope and technology. I became Muslim because there was actual proof.

In revisiting these proofs, I renew my faith that there is a Creator who has sent down messengers and books as a guidance for all people, with Muhammad (ﷺ) as the last guide for me. I renew my faith that when I pick up the Qur'an, I am reading the direct Words of the Creator of the Heavens and Earth. And my faith is renewed that there is an eternal life – there is Paradise. There is eternity in Paradise and that this is my sole aim – my sole goal – to live my life here in order to build my real estate there.

Realise this: you are here temporarily. You do not have one life. You have two: one life here as a means to take you there. Visualise Jannah – visualise yourself there. And use this life to work for what is permanent over that which is temporal.

The Messenger of Allah (ﷺ) said:

> Allah said, 'I have prepared for My pious worshippers such things as no eye has ever seen, no ear has ever heard and nobody has ever thought of. All that is reserved, besides which all that you have seen is nothing.'

Bukhari

Allah wants Jannah for you. Live life wanting it for yourself too.

Let Your Heart Ponder . . .

'Invest in this life in accordance with how long it will last; and invest in the Hereafter in accordance with how long it will last.'

Sufyan Ath-Thawri

'For the likes of this, let the workers work.'

Surah As-Saffat 37:61

'My Lord, grant me wisdom and unite me with the righteous, and grant me a reputation for truthfulness among the later generations. Make me one of the heirs of the Garden of Bliss.'

Surah Ash-Shuara 26:83–85

Du'a Invitation

My Perfect Lord, You have perfectly created a most Exquisite Permanent Home. Though my senses cannot perceive it, my belief in You and this deen produces an aching in my heart for it. It is a place of peace, joy, happiness and freedom. As I travel down this road of life, focus the eyes of my soul on what is ahead. There will be many distractions on my journey – remind me they are only distractions. Attach my heart to Your Gardens of Delight with such zeal that I align all that I am and everything I do with my ardent hope of being granted the keys to live there.

Journal

1. List three proofs from the Qur'an that really increase your faith in Allah, this deen and the akhirah.

....

....

....

2. Aside from meeting Allah, His Messenger and being with your family, what three things do you want to enjoy in Jannah?

....

....

....

3. Although Jannah is what eye has never seen and what the mind cannot comprehend, create a Jannah vision board.

....

....

....

My reflections
on the topic of The End are . . .

DAY 22

Dunya is a Means

When I was ten years old, I sat in a large chair next to my mother in front of my headmistress's desk. I was terrified. I kept racking my brain as to what I might have possibly done wrong at school to warrant my mother being called in. I wanted to ask her if Dad knew too – that would have meant greater problems!

The headmistress, Mrs Edwards, and my mother were catching up on school news and their love of classical music. My thoughts about the last few weeks' events were interrupted by Mrs Edwards's voice.

'Mrs Quadri, as you know, I've called you in to talk about your daughter.'

My mother side-eyed me but I couldn't read her expression.

'Yes, Mrs Edwards, has something happened?'

'I have something to show you,' Mrs Edwards said, pulling open the drawer of her mahogany desk. I gulped. She pulled out a black A4 book that looked familiar.

'Mrs Quadri, I would like you to have a read of this,' she said handing the book across the desk to my mother.

I watched my mother read the book and this time I could read her expression clearly.

'Mrs Quadri,' said my headmistress, 'I firmly believe one day your daughter will author and publish her own book. You ought to be proud.'

Immediately hearing those words, I sat up straight and in a matter of seconds, felt like I had grown taller. Mrs Edwards went on to explain how surprised the staff were by an amazing story I had written at such a young age.

It would be three decades later that I would be approached by my publisher to write the very book you are holding. In the space of those three decades came my conversion to Islam, years of heartache and difficulty, almost leaving Islam, returning to practise Islam, starting a family, founding a charity and in the midst of it all, one du'a – one hope – was repeatedly on my tongue: to write and publish a book before I left this world.

On this twenty-second day of Ramadan, I invite you to reflect back over the last twenty days. Billions of Muslims all around the world – from different nationalities, speaking different languages, breaking their fast with different food, and yet all doing so for the same reason – to attain taqwa, for the same Lord, Allah – with the hope of it being a means towards the same destination, Jannah.

We all have the same purpose to fulfil. And yet the path of our purpose is as individual and unique as our fingerprints. We all have an individual path to Allah ('azza wa jal). This is evident in the unique doors He opens for us and the ones He closes for us. It is evident in the types of tests He places on our path to bring us back to Him. It is also found in the worship we individually incline towards and the qualifications, skills and strengths we are uniquely blessed with.

On this twenty-second day of Ramadan, I want you to leave this chapter having an idea of how you would like to worship Him as you go into your future as your unique self. In addition, to craft how you wish to use this dunya as a means to journey to Him, exactly as you are.

I say as you are, because you are just right as you are. You can do wonderful things just as you are. You do not need to wait until your situation changes or until you learn this, lose weight, get married or have £20,000 in your bank account. You can make the most of what you have and who you are today.

We have been taught that when we ask for Jannah, we should ask for Firdous al ala (the best and highest level of Jannah). Take a lesson from this. This hadith teaches us that we need to aspire to great things. We are taught to hope for the absolute best; dream of the absolute best; settle for nothing less and do all that we can to achieve it.

You are and get what you focus on. Focus on Jannah. Choose your individual path to it carefully.

Dear reader, roll up your sleeves and let us get started – you are in the most blessed nights of the year, there is no better time to do this than now.

Firstly, I encourage you to make a du'a that I have repeatedly made for many, many years. But a warning, if you make it sincerely, be prepared for your life to change considerably. It is:

O Allah, you know me better than I know myself. I believe in Your Oneness. You know my strengths and my weaknesses, my sins and my good deeds. I live my life to serve and worship You. Use me, my Lord, for that which is pleasing to You. Use me in furthering this deen and ultimately bringing people back to Your Worship. I trust in You, Al-Aleem. I present myself fully to the ways in which You will answer this du'a and will do my utmost best to grab hold of the opportunities You bring my way. Forgive me and make me sincere. Use me for Your Sake, ya Rabbi.

You will soon start to brainstorm some important questions. But before you do that, know this: when you make this du'a sincerely, Allah will direct you in the best way to use you for His Sake. It may be as a mother or father to raise a child who will go on to do great things. It may be in supporting your neighbours, which will have a ripple effect for many family members. It may be in holding down the fort so that your spouse, sibling or child can go on to be successful. It may be in a business you run; it may be in charity work. It may be in writing a book. It may be in becoming an example for others because of what you went through. The share in the reward is the same. Trust Allah in how He chooses to use you – and note that this may change as you and your life change. Accept and respond, 'I am here, ya Rabbi.'

Just as we are all different, we also have different inclinations – and that is the case with worship too. Even when we read the seerah (life of the Prophet) and the lives of the companions of the Prophet (ﷺ), we find that some of them were known for giving sadaqa, others for the Qur'an, others for the night prayer and some for being able to forgive others. This is not to say they did not pursue other acts of worship, rather their hearts inclined towards one particular worship and they ran with it, excelled in it – and it became their individual path of worship to Allah.

What is yours? What act of worship, when you do it, fills you with a sweetness of faith and makes you want to do more of it – for no other reason than pleasing Allah, smiling at the thought of Him looking upon you Smiling? Write it down. Engage as much as possible in this act of worship. This will soften your heart and keep you in the mode of striving because it is something you enjoy doing. Now of course worship is not done for our own pleasure. But in a world where there is so much distraction and so much pulling us away from the path to Allah, worship you enjoy is a much needed starting point.

Next, what is an act of worship that you know would make a difference to your path to Allah ('azza wa jal), but you really struggle with? You want to do it. You know you need to. But it is like fighting yourself to actually do it. What is it? Write it down.

Know that this act of worship will be your means of taming your ego. By doing all that you can to accomplish it, you will be humbling yourself, disciplining yourself – which is necessary on this journey to Allah.

Now, we look at you and non-worship.

Who are you? What are you good at doing? What are the gifts that Allah has given to you? What makes you happy?

Sometimes, if our self-worth is low, we may find it difficult to answer these questions. If you struggle with them, a simple tip is to ask your nearest and dearest people to tell you what they believe you are good at and what skills and qualities Allah has gifted to you. Write them down.

Next, go back to the previous chapter and read the description of Jannah and the Day of Increase. Remember to use your senses to truly imagine the treasures of Jannah.

Dear reader, you only have one chance to build your permanent home in the next life. You only have one chance to use your skills in the path of Allah. You only have one chance to be loved by Allah. You only have one chance to leave a legacy of sadaqa jariah behind that will be of benefit to others and more so for you. You only have one chance to be blessed with the wonders of Jannah.

It is time to use your skills, strengths, gifts and abilities to make the most of your one chance.

On a blank page, write down your first immediate thoughts to this question: 'How can I use what I am good at in the dunya for the sake of my akhirah?' Go all out in answering this question. Dream big. If failure was not an option, what would you choose to do? Answer this question with all of the lessons you have taken from your past, be present and feel the possibility and believe Allah can make this possible for you.

Once you are done, thank your Lord – for Ar-Razzaq (The One who Provides) has just blessed you with an idea that may just transform your dunya and akhirah. Enjoy using the best time to make du'a during the remainder of these last ten nights to ask Allah to make this possible.

I leave you with this quote:

The Messenger of Allah (ﷺ) said, 'The best of what a man leaves behind are three: a righteous child who supplicates for him, ongoing charity the reward of which reaches him, and knowledge that is acted upon after him.'

Sunan Ibn Majah

Leave a legacy in this life for the eternal life. Let your light shine brightly after you have gone.

Let Your Heart Ponder . . .

'The Prophet (ﷺ) said, "A single endeavour or journey in the way of Allah is better than everything over which the sun rises and sets." In another narration, the Prophet said, "It is better than the world and everything in it."'

Bukhari and Muslim

Du'a Invitation

Al-Aleem, The All-Knowing, as I look ahead to the next life, I have a blank page to fill. I want to use what You have given to me and how You have fashioned me to leave behind a sadaqa jariah legacy that will benefit me in my grave. I ask You for Your help to fill this blank page. Direct me to what is best for me. Help me believe in my skills and abilities. Once I have begun to choose that which You know is best for me, attach my thoughts to it, to the point that the drive to bring it to reality occupies me. Grant me the determination and patience to bring it to reality.

Journal

1. If you have not done so already, complete the exercises in this chapter.

. . . .

. . . .

. . . .

. . . .

. . . .

2. Give yourself permission to feel excited – what could this mean for your dunya and akhirah? List all the wonderful benefits this could bring you in this life and the next.

. . . .

. . . .

. . . .

. . . .

. . . .

**My reflections
on the topic of
Dunya is a Means are . . .**

DAY 23

Tawakkul

I am not unaccustomed to taking big risks in my life – I embraced Islam at a young age and at a time when reverts were rare. I chose home education at a time when it was not the 'in thing'. I dived straight into the deep end and set up a charity from scratch. I moved from London to live in the Atlas Mountains. I moved back to the UK with nothing but my suitcase. And now this book. This book has literally had me feeling so nervous, so out of place. Imposter syndrome has been rife.

At different stages in the process of writing it, I have experienced anxiety. Thoughts like, 'I'm not a writer – I've never published a book before, what if it doesn't make sense?!' would send my heart racing.

Anxiety is a foreign feeling to me. Everything else I have ever done has made me feel nervous, yes, but never like an imposter, never anxious, never 'off'.

And so I got curious about this feeling and asked myself, 'Why am I feeling the way that I am? Is it because it's something new?' But then I realised, 'Everything else I have ever done was something new at the time, so it definitely cannot be that.' I sat with myself and kept asking myself, 'What is lying beneath these feelings of anxiety?'

I looked at all of the other things I have ever done and I finally found the anomaly. Everything else had been 'initiated by me', in the sense that Allah inspired me with the idea and I took steps to make the idea a reality. This book was not something I was looking for. Yes, I had been making du'a for it for years but it was not something I planned. It came from the Lord above the Heavens – and that scared the living daylights out of me.

Remember the story about my headmistress? I have been wanting this for decades! I started writing a book about my Shahaadah. I started writing a memoir about my life. But in all the crazy busyness of my life, Allah knew that it would only happen in the exact way that it has. And so here we are.

Feelings of doubt, nervousness and anxiety are natural feelings. They are not bad. They are not wrong.

When you choose Allah and His Paradise and make a conscious decision to heal to be present to work for Him, you will make big decisions that feel scary. And sometimes, like in my case, you will have dreams that you will plan, but He will Plan them way better and place you right in the thick of it so you have no choice but to make them a reality. Is this not love? Subhana'Allah.

When reading yesterday's chapter, you may have developed some seriously amazing ideas that feel scary. Perhaps you are worrying about how to turn these from ideas into reality. It's okay. Dream and intend, knowing that your intentions are rewarded even if they are not destined to manifest. Leave the how and when to the Best of Planners.

I once wrote down one of my dreams: to write a book that would draw hearts back to Allah ('azza wa jal). My vision was that it would be translated into lots of languages, reaching people in corners of the Earth that I had not visited. I still have that dream. I still have that intention. It feels scary to dream that big. But consider this: how many great things started as a seed in the mind of one person! You have every right to be that person too.

Dear reader, plant the seed and ask Allah to water it with you. Fear and anxiety are constructs of the mind based on the unknown. Feel them. Get curious about them and aim to understand where they are coming from.

With akhirah in mind, I want you to sit with your fears and concerns. If your dreams feel too big, ask yourself, 'Are they too big for Allah?' If you feel that you cannot do it, remind yourself you are in the Hands of Allah who can assist you in making it possible. If you feel that your current circumstances will not afford you the time to take the steps towards your dreams, remind yourself He is the One who can place barakah (blessings) on your time and perhaps take you away from your plans for a period of time to then suddenly force your dreams into existence, like He did in the case of my dream of writing a book.

You are a visitor in this dunya. And this dunya is one seriously scary place. People and experiences of the past can make you feel so unsure of the future. Perhaps you were always told, 'You'll never amount to anything', or maybe your experiences have thus far been of one door after another closing. All of this leads you to feel scared and anxious. It's okay. Breathe.

Tomorrow is a place you have not yet encountered. Yes, tomorrow is unknown. But you have a Lord who knows the ins and outs and intricacies of your tomorrow and who is guiding you every single moment of today in preparation for your tomorrow. He is a Lord who wants the best for you, and who will prepare your present for your future in the most perfect way. As the Qur'an reminds us:

> So why would we not put our trust in Allah when He has guided us on our paths to His Kindness.

> Surah Ibrahim 14:12

Place your plans and dreams behind your akhirah lens. Turn your dunya and akhirah dreams into a reality by traversing the journey with the One who Knows how and when best to get you there.

Dear reader, as you take steps towards the worship you wish to excel in, and the skills you will use to carve out a legacy for the sake of Allah, realise that your greatest tool is tawakkul – full reliance upon Allah ('azza wa jal).

Being akhirah-focused means being tawakkul-focused. Tawakkul grants you this feeling of strength because you know

Allah has your back. Tawakkul provides you the stability you need internally to carry out what you need to do externally. Tawakkul is you leaning against Allah when you feel like you cannot stand. Tawakkul is to lean on Allah in every state; relying on His Promise, surrendering to His Knowledge and being pleased with His Judgement. It is

> ... the heart's throwing of itself before the Lord as the dead body is thrown before the one who washes it, who turns it over as he pleases, or, giving up one's preference and going along with the flow of the decree.

> Ibn al-Qayyim, *Madaarij As-Salikeen*

The beauty of tawakkul is that with it comes this serene comfort, whereas anxiety simply produces discomfort and grief. If internal peace is not enough of a gift, then read these words of Ibn al-Qayyim:

> Whoever trusts in Allah in achieving something, he attains it.

> *Madaarij As-Salikeen*

Choose the path of tawakkul:

> Yahya bin Mu'adh was asked, 'When does a man attain true reliance?' He said, 'When he is pleased with Allah as the Disposer of Affairs.'

> *Madaarij As-Salikeen*

Dear reader, I invite you to think about someone in your life that you turn to for help. What qualities make you so sure you can lean on them? How do you know they possess such qualities? It is because you know them and you know they can be relied upon, no matter what. The number one way to develop strong tawakkul is to invest time in getting to know your Creator by studying His Names and Attributes. Know Him and you will develop the best of thoughts about Him. You will know He will never let you down. As Ibn al-Qayyim said:

> The more you have good expectations of your Lord and hope in Him, the more you will rely on and trust in Him. This is why some have explained true reliance and trust as having good expectations of Allah. In truth, having good expectations of Him leads to relying on and trusting in Him, as it is impossible that one can trust in someone that he has bad expectations of or no hope in.

Madaarij As-Salikeen

As you step into your future, I invite you to internalise Allah's Name and Attribute, Al-Wakil. Al-Wakil is the One to whom you entrust the care and management of your life to. Al-Wakil is the Guardian of your best interests. Al-Wakil is the One to rely upon. Al-Wakil is your Representative and steps in when you are incapable, in the best of ways. You are not alone. You are protected by the Best Protector.

Lean fully against your Lord.

Let Your Heart Ponder . . .

'Whoever places his heart with his Lord will be in tranquillity and relaxation. And whoever sends his heart to the people will be struck by calamities and will increase in sadness and anxiety.'

Ibn al-Qayyim, *Al Fawaa'id*

'If you were to trustingly rely on God the right way He would feed you as He feeds the bird that leaves hungry in the morning and returns in the evening with a full stomach.'

Sunan Tirmidhi

Du'a Invitation

Al-Wakil, my dreams feel scary. I worry I can't do this. I feel anxious it won't materialise. I acknowledge I can never rely on my imperfect self. I choose instead to rely upon You. I am leaning on You for You know how best to support me. You fulfil Your Promises and so I trust You. You are The Most Able, so when I am weak and confused, I rely on You to strengthen me and guide my way. I do not know the future so I trust in Your Knowledge, which encompasses absolutely everything. Al-Wakil, when I forget, remind me to rely on You. Instil within me a trust of You and a reliance upon You that resembles the tawakkul my Prophet (ﷺ) had with You:

O Allah, unto You I surrender, in You I believe, on You I trustingly rely, to You I turn, with Your help I contend with my adversaries. O Allah, I seek refuge in Your Might: there is no God but You, lead me not astray! You are the Alive who dies not, and jinn and humankind die.

Bukhari and Muslim

Journal

1. What are your three main worries about the path to turning your dunya dreams into a reality?

....

....

....

....

2. Take them to Allah with full reliance and surrender. Having done so, how do you feel?

....

....

....

....

3. The last time I relied upon Allah felt . . .

....

....

....

....

**My reflections
on the topic of Tawakkul are . . .**

DAY 24

Hope

Returning to the birthing story I mentioned in Day 15, in February 2010, my pre-labour contractions started at thirty-seven weeks. I began to despair a little as the experience seemed to be so similar to my previous pregnancy. I started to have irregular contractions that were painful and which would sometimes become regular. This went on for roughly two weeks. I did not go near the hospital as I knew that my chance of having a VBA2C (vaginal birth after two caesareans) would be taken away from me if I entered hospital in pre-labour. So, I dealt with the pain at home.

On Saturday, 27 February 2010, I heard news that a dear sister who was also attempting a VBA2C had given birth by caesarean. She had tried so hard, but in this instance the section was needed. I felt happy for her that she had given it her best shot but I felt somewhat despondent as to whether I could actually do this. I was tired and the pre-labour was taking a lot out of me. I remember crying as I called a dear sister for support. She gave me advice which I honestly believe contributed towards the wonderful experience that I had. She told me to reconnect with Allah, to turn to Him, to really pour my heart out to Him and to remember that the outcome of this was really in His Hands. And so, after finishing the call, I made wudu (ablution) – paying attention to each part of the process. I prayed two raka'at (units of prayer) and made a very lengthy du'a.

I asked Allah to make me content with His decree. I asked

Him to grant me this VBA2C if it was good for me. I asked Him to make me strong. I made a lot of istighfaar and I tried to use the best ways to make du'a; facing the qiblah – praying in the direction of the Kaaba in the Sacred Mosque in Makkah – imploring Him using His Most Beautiful Names and Attributes, repeating my requests three times, sending salawaat (peace and blessings) on the Prophet. I kept repeating the same phrase over again and again, 'I know You can do this, Allah. I know You will grant me what is best. This is easy for You. I know You can and I know You will.'

After I finished supplicating, I felt ready for whatever He would bring my way. I felt ready for even a repeat caesarean because I knew that I had done everything I could to plan for this VBA2C, and I had asked Him – it was now in His Hands. I had spoken to Him with intense hope.

A few hours later, my midwife told me to catch my baby, after he entered the birthing pool without tearing my old scar and, Alhamdulillah, there were no complications.

It has been many years since I have recounted this story and now, thirteen years since my son's birth, the memories of that day leave me feeling very emotional.

Today a friend shared something she recently heard: 'The days are long but the years are short.' How true this is – that time flies by so quickly that we forget the situations when we needed hope, when we called upon Him with hope and when He heard us and turned to us. It is important to revisit previous memories, especially as we embark upon our future, as they can fill us to the brim with hope.

Tawakkul preceded this chapter as once you rely upon Allah and hand Him the keys to your life and declare, 'Ya Rabbi, do whatever You will because I know what You will do is absolutely best', it is then that you march forth with absolute hope. Hope is the other wing of the bird analogy by Ibn al-Qayyim. Hope is needed for us to fly to Allah. There is a beautiful verse in the Qur'an where Allah ('azza wa jal) says:

> Whosoever expects to meet his Lord, let him do righteous works and never associate anyone in the worship of his Lord.

Surah Kahf 18:110

Can you imagine meeting the One you prayed to, fasted for, cried to, implored, begged and withheld for? Can you imagine being denied meeting Him as a result of what your own hands put forth? I cannot imagine going through this dunya if deprived of being in His Loving Presence.

What I love about this verse from the eighteenth chapter of the Qur'an, is that although hope resides within, it is to be manifested outwardly. To hope is to do, to move, to act. If you really have hope that you will meet your Beloved, then it is time to get up and worship and work hard.

Hope brings a sweetness to this dunya. Hope keeps us alive while so much may be dying around us and sometimes within us.

I have always wondered where I would be and how I would manage the nature of this dunya without hope in Allah. Quite frankly, I feel I would die before my death.

In the last few days, you have readjusted your lens to become akhirah-focused. Your worship has been refined through that lens. You have given yourself permission to dream about how you can use your unique skills and attributes to be successful in this dunya for the ultimate success of the akhirah. You have wondered how it will all come to be. You have placed your trust in your Lord who says, 'Be.' And it is.

Hope must now follow. Roll up your sleeves and take steps towards your vision with full expectation that not only will He bring about your vision but that He will do so with abundant blessings. He is as you think Him to be.

Al-Karim – Allah is so Generous. He awakens us to our priority. He shifts our heart towards Him and makes us concerned about that which will benefit us in the long term and fills us with a sweetness in the short term. He then guides us to see how we can worship Him better. He reminds us of who we are, so we can use our gifts to increase and elevate our rank in the Hereafter and then He gives us the means to work hard with hope for Him! Allahu Akbar! (Allah is Greater than everything.)

A person who follows up tawakkul with hope does so because he or she understands the vastness of His Love and Mercy.

The Messenger of Allah (ﷺ) said,

> Allah Almighty said: 'O son of Adam, if you call upon Me and place your hope in Me, I will forgive you despite what is within you and I will not hesitate. O son of Adam, if you have sins piling up to the clouds and then ask for My forgiveness, I will forgive you without hesitation. O son of Adam, if you come to Me with enough sins to fill the earth and then you meet Me without associating anything with Me, I will come to you with enough forgiveness to fill the earth.'

> Sunan Tirmidhi

> I am as my servant thinks I am. I am with him. Whenever he mentions Me to himself, I mention him to Myself. When he mentions Me in a company, I mention him in a company better than them. If he draws near to Me, by a hand-span, I draw near to him by a fathom (the length of outspread arms). And if he comes to Me walking, I come to him running.

> Muslim

When you place your hopes completely in Allah and you have absolute faith in Him – and you follow that up with action, He will respond with a return that is far better. Every time.

Whatever your position is, whether you are hoping that He

will help you heal from your past, or have hope in Him assisting you in being present or hope that He will guide you to live out your plans for the akhirah – know that true hope manifests into action.

Your actions reflect the hope you place in Allah. And the level of hope you have depends on your love for Him. A true lover hopes for His Beloved before they are reunited. And when he or she is in the presence of the Beloved, hope in Him only develops further.

Hope is everything on this journey to Allah. We have hope we will be forgiven. We have hope that Allah will help us change. We have hope that our worship and effort will be accepted.

I leave you with the words of Ibn al-Jawzi:

He whose Kindness manifests when He is Angry, How do you imagine He is when He is pleased?

Sayd al-Khater

I have full hope in Your Love and Mercy.

Let Your Heart Ponder . . .

'Yahya ibn Abi Kathir reported: Umar ibn al-Khattab, may Allah be pleased with him, said, "If a caller from heaven announced that all people would enter Paradise together but for one man, I would fear that I am him. And if a caller announced that all people would enter Hellfire together but for one man, I would hope that I am him."'

Ḥilyat al-Awliyā'

'My Lord, the dearest of Your gifts in my heart is hope in You, the sweetest words upon my tongue are Your praise, the most beautiful of my hours is one in which I meet You.'

Yahya bin Mu'adh, quoted in *Madaarij As-Salikeen*

Du'a Invitation

Ar-Rahman, The Most Merciful, the first verse in the first surah of the Qur'an reads, 'In the name of Allah, The Entirely Merciful, The Especially Merciful'. The Qur'an, Your Perfect Words, which starts with these words is a reminder to me to be ever hopeful of You. How can I not have hope in You, when You have created me, nourished me, supported me and guided me. You are a Lord who has created a Paradise for the little imperfect good deeds that Your servants do. You have created an eternity of peace and joy for the small time I was present in this life. How can I not have hope in You. I walk into my future with the best opinion of You, with full hope that my life will align with my desire to meet You and live underneath Your Glorious Throne.

Journal

1. Write one statement of hope next to each of your plans for your akhirah-focused future.

....

....

....

....

2. The last time I had hope in Allah was when . . .

....

....

....

....

3. This led to . . .

....

....

....

....

**My reflections
on the topic of Hope are . . .**

DAY 25

Du'a

I am a firm believer in du'a. Life experiences have taught me to make du'a from a position of 'when' and not 'if'. And this is what I want you to take away from today's chapter. While I have many du'a stories from my own life that I could share, I am finding it difficult to pick one. So the du'a I will share concerns a dear friend's younger sister.

My friend made a request for du'a on a WhatsApp group in the middle of last year. Her sister had been married for twelve years but was unable to conceive. There were a dozen or so replies with du'a for her sister. A year later, my dear friend announced that her sister had given birth. All of us on the group were in complete and utter shock. I personally remember thinking it felt like only yesterday that the du'a request had been made.

Immediately, I wondered – who amongst us might be an awliya (close friend) of Allah? Whose du'a perhaps reached our Lord upon His Throne, above the heavens? Who has a heart that is so pure that their du'a was answered so quickly? Subhan'Allah. Or could it be that when my friend told her sister a group of women on the other side of the world were making du'a for her, this increased her faith, gave her a boost and helped her make a different, more intense du'a that was accepted?

On this journey of taqwa, du'a is everything. How can we become conscious of Allah if we do not know Him? How can we know Him if we do not speak to Him, call upon and ask of

Him? How can we navigate this journey to the akhirah without asking Him to guide our way? How do we cope with the nature of this journey without complaining to Him, thanking Him for relief and telling Him about our days?

A relationship is built through time, communication and intimacy. The intimacy with Allah is found in du'a. It is a private sitting with the King of Kings where you come vulnerable before Him, asking Him for whatever your heart desires.

For anyone who craves this level of intimacy with our Beloved, know it only comes from Allah being the focus in the ordinary moments of our lives so that we may bask in the very intimate moment of du'a. When we have a connection with Allah for every experience we encounter in this dunya, we will find ourselves naturally turning to Him. We receive something and thank Him. We lose something, we ask Him for assistance. We hurt, we ask Him for relief. We are excited, we share our joy and praise Him. We are nervous, we ask Him, 'Be with me.' This is du'a. This is relationship. This is what builds intimacy. We need not think we have to be pious Muslims 'close to perfection' in order to experience a special relationship with Allah. This special connection is available to everyone.

Any type of relationship becomes special depending on the effort we put into it. And we can do this as we go about our everyday life.

In the early years of my being a Muslim, I attended an Islamic lecture. I cannot remember most of what was said, but one statement has stayed with me over twenty years later. The speaker said, 'In the month of Ramadan, when you have a date, wanting to get the reward of feeding a fasting person, with the dates between your fingers – pause before you offer it to someone, and say to Allah, "This is for You."' Doing this regularly will produce within you a feeling that cannot be described in words. It reminds me of a beautiful quote that I came across online:

Do not let the heavens miss your voice, be a servant whom the angels know by your supplication, when you utter your demands and they say, 'Our Lord, it is a well-known voice from a well-known slave.'

May we be of them! Ameen.

Here we are, Day 25 of Ramadan with only a few days left. It does not matter how you have spent the last twenty-five days or the last five of these blessed last ten nights. Whatever worship you have or have not done, make the remaining days of Ramadan an intimate time between you and your Lord by talking to Him.

Let me share one of the most beautiful verses of the Qur'an with you. In Surah Baqarah, verse 186, Allah ('azza wa jal) says,

> When My servants ask you about Me, I am near. I answer the prayer of the prayerful whenever he prays to Me.

When the Prophet (ﷺ) was asked by his people about all types of matters – from questions about the crescent moon in verse 189 in Surah Baqarah to a question about the sacred months in verse 217 – Allah would respond through revelation upon Muhammad (ﷺ) with 'Qul', meaning 'Tell them', followed by the answer. However, the verse quoted above is different. In this verse, there is a linguistic beauty in how Allah responds. He ('azza wa jal) says, 'When My servants ask you about Me, I am near.' 'Qul' meaning 'Tell them' is removed, linguistically removing Muhammad (ﷺ) from the response just as he is removed from the direct intimate connection experienced between servant and Lord in du'a. There is no intermediary. We have a direct line to Allah.

Dear reader, know whatever from your past needs healing or rectifying, whatever you need help with to become more present, whatever you need on this journey of taqwa and the yearning in your heart for your worship and dunya dreams to manifest, know one thing – He is Near.

In these last few days left of Ramadan, as you ask Allah for all that you want for your akhirah-focused future, upgrade your du'a in these respects:

1. Make du'a from a place of vulnerability and absolute need. Sometimes, the only du'a you can make is exclaiming 'Allah' with desperation.

2. Begin by praising Allah and sending salawaat (peace and blessings upon the Prophet). Remember: 'Every supplication is screened until the salah is sent upon the Prophet' (Al-Albani).

3. Be certain when you make du'a. There should be no 'Allah, please', or 'My Rabb, if you can'. The Messenger of Allah (ﷺ) said: 'Let not any of you say: "O Allah! Forgive me if You wish. O Allah! Show me mercy if You wish. Rather, ask from Allah with certitude for no one has the power to compel Allah"' (Bukhari and Muslim).

4. Accustom yourself to speaking to Allah during good times as well as at times of need. Know that: 'Whoever desires that Allah answers him in times of hardship and distress, then he should be plentiful in supplicating to Him in times of hardship' (Sunan Tirmidhi).

5. Call upon Allah using His Beautiful Names and Attributes, for: 'And to Allah belong the Most Beautiful Names, so use them to call upon Him' (Surah Al-Araf 7:180).

6. Cry to him at one of the best times du'a is answered – in the last third of the night. This is when we have been told that Allah descends and asks the angels, 'Who of

my servants are asking of me, so that I may respond to them?' Imam Shafi said, 'The du'a made at tahajjud is like an arrow that does not miss its target.' If there is something you want so very much, you need to ask yourself a simple question: why am I not waking up for tahajjud (prayer at the last part of the night) and making du'a for it?

7. Attach your du'a to the du'a of Prophet Yunus (peace be upon him):

The Messenger of Allah (ﷺ) said, 'The supplication of Yunus, when he called upon Allah inside the belly of the whale was this, "There is no God but You, Glory be to You for I have certainly been among the wrongdoers" (21:87). Verily, a Muslim never supplicates for anything with it but that Allah will answer him.'

Sunan Tirmidhi

8. Dear reader, after you have called upon your Lord, have full hope in His Response. The Prophet (ﷺ) said,

'. . . There is no Muslim who calls upon Allah, without sin or cutting family ties, but that Allah will give him one of three answers: He will quickly fulfil his supplication, He will store it for him in the Hereafter, or He will divert an evil from him similar to it.' They said, 'In that case we will ask for more.' The Prophet said, 'Allah has even more.'

Musnad Aḥmad

And after you have done all of this; after you have poured out your heart to Allah whether in a state of joy, need or desperation, recall this beautiful reminder from Umar ibn al-Khattab (may Allah be pleased with him), who said:

> I am not worried about whether my du'a will be responded to, but rather, I am worried about whether I will be able to make du'a or not. So, if I have been guided (by Allah) then (I know) that the response will come with it.

Be greedy with Allah. You are asking Al-Kareem – The Most Generous.

Let Your Heart Ponder . . .

'Your voice, which you think does not go beyond the ceiling, goes beyond the seven skies (indeed, He is Hearing and Near). Maybe Allah is delaying your response as He loves to hear your voice.'

Anon

'You are a servant who has forgotten what you have asked from Allah, The Most High. You have a Lord who turns to you sometimes years later, granting you what you asked for – showing you He hears and never forgets.'

Aliyah Umm Raiyaan

'Say, "Indeed, my prayer, my rites, and my way of living and my way of dying are for Allah, Lord of the realms. No associate is there for Him. And to this I have been commanded, and I am the first [among you] of the Muslims . . . "'

Surah Al-An'am 6:162–163

Du'a Invitation

Al-Mujeeb, The One who Responds, I yearn to pass through this life close to You. I wish to communicate with You more than I speak with anyone else. I desire to turn to You first before anyone else. I want to acknowledge You before I acknowledge anyone else. Attach my soul to its dialogue with You. Fill my days with praise for You, sharing my concerns with You and asking of You. And when I speak with You, place within my heart certainty that You hear me. Guide me to be persistent and consistent in my du'a. And when You grant me this and more, humble me to make du'a to You, thanking You for permitting it all.

Journal

1. Remind yourself of a time when Allah answered your du'a. How did it feel?

....

....

....

....

2. Apply some of the suggested ways to upgrade your du'a to your akhirah-focused goals.

....

....

....

....

3. Take ten minutes out and simply talk to Allah.

....

....

....

....

My reflections
on the topic of Du'a are . . .

DAY 26

Patience

There are two people in my life who have been tested relentlessly. They have been dealt with one big test followed by many others. I look at these two souls and my heart breaks for them at the pain they have had to endure. But it also breaks in joy for them as I know Allah must love them beyond what their hearts could ever imagine.

To protect their privacy, I will not go into great detail about their tests. However, I can tell you that between the two of them, they have been tested with abusive partners, divorce, a child who was sexually abused and as a result self-harmed and attempted suicide, and the death of a child from terminal illness; they have faced slander and lies, the loss of property, children that have unjustly been taken away from them; going through the court system to fight for justice against a child abuser; and being granted ease through remarriage – only to lose their beautiful spouse in sudden death. One cannot imagine two people going through all of this along with the emotions, trauma and heartbreak that result from such trials.

I have never observed patience in the way that these two servants of Allah have displayed it. Where they could have retaliated, they did not. Where they could have proven the truth to their community, they chose to be content with their Lord knowing the truth. Where they could have despaired, they trusted Allah. Where they could have fallen apart, they were patient.

I have personally witnessed both cry. I have heard directly from both how painful these tests have been for them. I have witnessed them withdraw into silence when it all became too much.

Yet I have never once heard them complain or ask 'Why?' Instead, statements such as 'I trust my Lord'; 'As long as I am not the oppressor and Allah is pleased with me, Alhamdulillah'; 'I will take it to the next life'; 'Allah sees'; 'Allah knows' and 'He is the Best of Planners' have escaped their lips.

Their patience can only be described as 'sabrun jameel' – the most beautiful patience for enduring circumstances that had been predestined for them. They were patient in being content with Allah's Decree, knowing their adversities were purifying them, helping them turn to Allah and feel closer to Him. They were patient in surrendering to His will. They were patient in complaining to Him. They were patient in being grateful to Him for the good and the bad.

Allah says,

> And those who are patient in affliction and loss, and at the utmost moment of calamity – such are the truthful and such are the God-conscious.

> Surah Baqarah 2:177

Now, here I am describing patience associated with great trials. And I chose to do so to show you that if people in such dire circumstances can be patient, then we too can be patient with our own burdens and our lighter challenges too.

Patience is possible when Allah ('azza wa jal) bestows it on a person. The Messenger of Allah (ﷺ) said,

> Whoever would be patient, then Allah will make him patient. No one is given a gift that is better and more comprehensive than patience.

> Bukhari and Muslim

I sat with this hadith and thought really hard about the times when I have been impatient, and something occurred to me: I had been so focused on the challenge and difficulty, that patience as an option did not even occur to me. Interestingly, the two servants of Allah I mentioned at the beginning had chosen patience at some point during their tests and Allah blessed them with even more patience.

Now, patience did not mean they sat and prayed in a corner about the injustice they and their families encountered. It did not mean they did not seek justice. I know both fought for justice probably harder than anyone else I know. But within that they were patient in their reliance upon Allah. They understood this was their qadr. They understood Allah tests those He Loves. They accepted His Decree and they leant on Him through it all and were patient in their leaning, waiting for a solution, relief and ease to arrive. This was their patience.

Dear reader, as you work towards your akhirah-focused future goals, speaking to Allah, facing challenges with trust in Him, translating that into hope manifested into action – the next step is to be patient.

You need to be patient with yourself. Some days, despite your efforts, will not go to plan. You need to trust when Allah intervenes and turns your plans upside down, placing you on a different path. You need to be patient for the answer to your du'a. You need to be patient when you feel you are doing this alone, unsupported.

You need to choose patience because patience is always needed on any journey and this journey of God-consciousness is the most intense, most surprising, most beautiful and yet testing journey of them all. Know when you choose patience, really choose it from deep within, know 'Allah is with the patient' (Surah Anfaal 8:46). Know that choosing patience leads you to His Love, for 'Allah loves the patient' (Surah Al-Imran 3:146). Know that choosing patience is better for you in the long term for 'if you remain patient, that is better for those who are patient' (Surah An-Nahl 16:126).

The path to becoming more patient is found in pushing against what your ego is calling to, planting a seed of patience and having full hope Allah will water it and let it grow.

It is found in feeling through the difficulty with Allah while also contemplating how it could have been worse. It is turning to Allah and telling Him, 'This is hard', while considering the hardships of others which are more severe. It is being aware of how painful it is to live through such difficulty while focusing on the hope that this trial will lead to great reward in the Permanent Life.

It is found in certitude that this too will pass.

It was said, 'How do we observe patience when every ounce of your existence is screaming to give up?' The sheikh beautifully phrased the answer saying, 'In the same manner that we fast; completely certain that the adhaan of maghrib will eventually be called.'

Choose a beautiful patience.

Let Your Heart Ponder . . .

'Believers, find strength through patience and prayer. Allah is with those who are patient.'

Surah Baqarah 2:153

'Our Lord! Pour out patience upon us, and take us at death as Muslims.'

Surah Al-Araf 7:126

Du'a Invitation

Allah, You are Patient with me. When I intend that I will and don't, You patiently wait until I do. When I make mistakes, do better and make mistakes again, You patiently observe me as I continue to trip and fall. When You gift me and I forget to thank You, You patiently wait for my gratitude. You are The Most Patient. Turn my heart into a patient one. When I ask of You, help me to be patient for Your response, when Your Plan takes over my own, fill me with patience to accept that which I cannot change. As I aim to work towards an akhirah-focused future, remind me that You are Patient with me and so I must be patient with myself in living for You.

Journal

1. Write down a time when you were impatient. How did it feel?

....

....

....

2. How did it affect you and others?

....

....

....

3. How can you be patient as you continue on your journey of God-consciousness to Allah?

....

....

....

4. The next time I am impatient, I will immediately do the following . . .

....

....

....

**My reflections
on the topic of Patience are . . .**

DAY 27

Istikharaa

My daughter was fourteen at the time. We were living in a village in the Atlas Mountains in Algeria and she was completely overwhelmed with her studies. Prior to moving to Algeria when she was ten years old, she had been home-educated in the UK. When we moved to Algeria she entered the Algerian public school system for a number of years while still being home-schooled with the British curriculum. It was a lot for her to take on – particularly as she moved closer to exam time for both systems.

I remember her coming home from school one day with her heavy rucksack, flinging off her boots and crying her eyes out. The amount of homework, tests, Qur'an revision and British home education was weighing down heavily on her. We had left the UK with nothing to return to, so our home and the continuation of her education looked to be permanently based in Algeria. However, we had discussed keeping her options open should she ever want to return to the UK and pursue further education once she had completed a degree in Algeria one day in the future.

With her head in her hands, she looked at me, confused.

I went to my eldest child and said, 'Weigh up the pros and cons of continuing with your GCSEs or stopping them. Sit with your list. Speak to a few people here and a few people there in the UK. Once you've weighed up your options and chosen which path you would like to take, you must lift it up to Allah through salatul istikharaa (the prayer for guidance). Your Lord knows your future. Should you be blessed with life, He knows exactly what is going to happen to you and for you in ten, twenty years from now. So call upon Him and ask Him to guide you. Do it. Be certain He will guide you to what is best. Whichever path you choose, if it is good for you, He will facilitate it. If it is bad for you, He will block it.'

She looked at me, nodded and a few days later prayed the prayer of istikharaa on the decision of continuing with her GCSEs.

A few years later, her father and I divorced. On a visit to the UK, I got stuck there due to Covid-19 lockdown restrictions. The months away from my children were unbearable. They managed to get onto a repatriation flight to visit me for what we thought would only be a few months until we could all return to Algeria, but the borders in Algeria remained closed and there was no way for us to return home. I've mentioned earlier in this book how in December 2020, four months after they arrived in the UK, the Algerian home that we spent years building burnt down, destroying all of our possessions.

As I write this book, it has been two years since my children returned on that repatriation flight. We are now living in the UK. My daughter completed her GCSEs as a home-schooled student and is currently in her last year of A-Levels and applying to university.

Allah knows our future. It is time to move towards fulfilling the du'a you decided upon on Day 22.

I have a friend who jokes and says my life motto is: Decision. Dua. Move. And it is true. I am a lover of istikharaa. I believe in it. I use it and I cannot live without it.

Dear reader, Allah ('azza wa jal) has given us a most precious gift – the prayer where we seek guidance. It is a gift because it works every single time! Every time. Now, contrary to some belief, it has nothing to do with a feeling or seeing a dream as an answer to which decision you should take. It has everything to do with the facilitation or blocking of the very decision you have prayed upon.

Allah wants you to move and keep moving. Stagnation is not part of our journey of taqwa. Rest, yes. Rejuvenate, of course. But definitely not stagnation.

To move into your akhirah-focused future, istikharaa must become your compass. Whether it is do with your dunya dreams, a major life decision, minor everyday decisions or just something you are confused about, I advise you to use istikharaa.

When you feel stuck, not knowing which of two paths (or more!) to take, place the options under your akhirah-focused lens. Then look ahead to what will aid you most in the next life.

A dilemma is often the worst position to be in. It feels so heavy. Whichever way you look, you see potential benefits and harm. Before you take a step, pause and ask yourself a simple question: What would be most pleasing to Allah and most beneficial to my next life? Looking at the dilemma with that perspective provides you with the best choice to take.

Make wudu and pray your two raka'at with sincerity, humility, deep desperation for a response and finally, with yaqeen (certainty) that you will be shown very clearly whether this is good or bad for your dunya and akhirah.

Istikharaa is a tool that calms us. We are able to lift the heaviness of our dilemma up to the All-Knowing. By praying istikharaa, we are translating belief into practice. How? We are conversing with our Lord who already Knows which path is best. He Knows whether the decision we take will materialise or not and whether that will lead us to good or harm. Through istikharaa, we come to Allah admitting our weakness – that we have no clue what to do because our knowledge is limited to the present moment – and we testify to His Supreme Knowledge of all that the future holds.

By voluntarily placing our head on the ground, followed by the most beautiful testimony of trust and submission, we testify that we are confident in His Perfect Knowledge of what He already knows will or will not come to pass, and what will or will not be best for us. We plead with Him to ease our worries and to guide us to that which is best. Our bodies and tongues articulate a level of trust in Him that is the most perfect prescription for our anxiety and worry. The entire experience is called submission. And at that point we become true believers.

Istikharaa does not end there. Yes, you have made a decision and taken it to Allah through prayer but there is something you now need to do, which most fail to do. You need to move immediately.

You have made a decision. You have lifted it up to the Lord of the Worlds – but you cannot sit and wait for the answer to fall from the sky. This is not faith. It is time to take action towards the very decision you made immediately, with all your senses on red alert as to whether Allah is blocking or facilitating the decision you presented to Him.

Post istikharaa, our eyes look out for the signs. Is Allah making the path of my decision easy? Is He bringing me to it and bringing it to me? Or is He distancing me from it and it from me?

Sometimes the answer appears blurred because we are seeing what we want to see rather than seeing what He wants us to see. Istikharaa is an act of submission and trust. Post istikharaa, there is a much needed lesson in humility: to step back and allow Him to guide our eyes and heart to perceive His Signs; His Guidance; His Answer.

By placing our ego aside, we allow ourselves a glimpse of how His Knowledge manifests perfectly in our brief lives. With certainty, His Answer is always best and blessed, even if His answer is the very opposite of what you had decided upon and wanted.

There are times when istikharaa can be as clear as a blue sky, with bright shining stars revealing the best path to follow. Other times the sky is so cloudy, you can just about make out the light of the moon peeking through the dark grey clouds – only for it to leave as quickly as it came; gone. And you wonder if it was a figment of your imagination; your mind desperately wanting to see a sign that in fact, perhaps, was never there.

This waiting period of istikharaa is one where we can become so fixated on the waiting, the looking and the searching for signs and His answer that we forget we still need to live life.

The answer to istikharaa is that your Lord, Most High, facilitates your decision by making the path easy towards your decision. It is smooth sailing. He brings it to you and brings you to it. Or Allah shows you that this is not best for you, and as you take steps towards it, you are prevented from obtaining it and it is prevented from reaching you. Hope is provided for the seeker with the supplication asking for that which is better and a contentment with it.

The true beauty of istikharaa is that if your decision is facilitated, Allah provides an extra bundle of barakah with it. I have experienced this every single time. We have a Lord who not only directs us to what is best but then increases us when it is.

When I started my charity, Solace UK, I prayed istikharaa for it to go ahead and immediately emailed twenty sisters about my idea to see who might be interested. Hardly any responded. Some even mocked me. But those who did became part of the foundation of Solace.

When I had the idea for the YouTube show *Honest Tea Talk*, I prayed istikharaa and approached my two co-hosts. After our initial meeting, we all prayed istikharaa and then due to a lack of financial backing for this start-up, put our own money towards filming the first three episodes. Within a couple of months, *HTT* aired and it very quickly reached thousands of views. All praise and thanks are due to Him.

When I was approached by my publisher to write this book, after our initial conversation, I prayed istikharaa and immediately took my pen and notebook to a local park where I brainstormed a book outline and what each chapter would entail. After it was presented at an acquisition meeting – and subsequently an offer was made to me – I accepted, Alhamdulilllah. And here you are holding that very book!

I share these examples from my own life to show you the power of istikharaa and the Power of Allah ('azza wa jal).

Remember to move quickly after istikharaa – for how will you see the answer if you remain still? He always wants you to move. For life is a journey towards Him, towards death, towards another life and a final home for eternity near Him. A journey always requires movement. Decide with Him. Lift it up to Him. Trust in Him. Move with Him.

Decision. Istikharaa. Move.

Let Your Heart Ponder . . .

'Ibn Abi Jamra (Allah have mercy upon Him), a great scholar, said, "The wisdom behind putting the ṣalāh before the istikhārah is the istikhārah combines both the good of this world and the next. Just like in this dunya a person needs to go to the one he needs something from and win his favour and then put his need before them, the ṣalāh preceding the supplication is like knocking at the door of the King and presenting yourself before Allāh (subḥānahu wa ta'āla) and making sujūd and humbling yourself and putting your face on the ground before Allāh and then spreading your hands and presenting your need before Allāh (subḥānahu wa ta'āla)."'

Abdul Nasir Jangda, *Istikharaa: how to and why*

Du'a Invitation

'O Allah, I seek guidance from Your Knowledge and Power from Your Might, and I ask You from Your tremendous favour. Verily, You have Power and I do not have Power, and You know and I do not know. You are the Knower of the unseen. O Allah, if You know that this matter is good for my religion and my livelihood and my fate, or if it is better for my present and latter needs, then decree it for me and make it easy for me and bless me in it. But if You know that this matter is evil for my religion and my livelihood and my fate, or if it is worse for my present and latter needs, then divert it from me and keep me away from it, and decree what is good for me and then make me content with it.'

Translation of the istikharaa prayer

Journal

1. Consider the legacy you have been working on in the last few days. Thereafter, journal how you feel.

....

2. Write down any other life dilemmas you are currently in.

....

3. Place all options behind your akhirah-focused lens.

....

4. Speak to people who are qualified or experienced in the area of those options, weighing up the pros and cons.

....

5. Make a decision.

....

6. Pray istikharaa.

....

7. Now take immediate steps in the direction of that decision.

....

8. Write down how you feel.

....

**My reflections
on the topic of Istikharaa are . . .**

DAY 28

Private Deeds

On this Day 28, I need to tell you about a sister called Amina. Amina is a simple soul. Her character makes her one of the most beautiful people I know.

Amina loves Allah very much. Her knowledge in Islam is average. She recites Qur'an very slowly – struggling to join each letter to the next. The special thing about Amina is that she really does love her Lord.

Amina said something to me many years ago that nestled itself within my mind and would not leave. I kept replaying her words again and again and they reminded me of a hadith that mentioned ordinary companions of the Prophet (ﷺ) who were guaranteed Jannah. They were simple beings like you and I but their actions and motives were pure, untainted by riyaa (pride) or any other worldly reason. That simple deed or part of their character created their path to Jannah.

One day I asked Amina how, without fail, she would always keep to the sunnah fasts throughout the year – hardly missing any. Now, the only reason why I knew that she was fasting was that she would be the only one who would regularly decline food or a cup of tea when we and other home-educating mothers would gather. She would fast on Mondays, Thursdays, the three white days and the other highly recommended sunnah fasts throughout the year. She hardly missed any fasts except when she was on her monthly cycle. In the freezing winter, when her body called for the warmth of a hot drink, or in the scorching summer heat, when it craved ice-cold drinks, she still was not tempted away from fasting for her Lord.

She replied to my question with a sigh, 'Aliyah, I wish I could do more for Allah. I don't know very much and I don't have control over finances in our home, so can't give sadaqa as I'd like to. But I hope that, through fasting, Allah will accept me as His Slave.'

Her words exuded sincerity. She knew that this was some-thing she could give to Allah easily and consistently in the hope that she would be counted amongst His sincere slaves. Her words still amaze me to this day. She chose an act of ibadah that hardly anyone else would know about and has held on to it with dear life all these years. Her book of good deeds is full of one of the best deeds.

The Messenger of Allah (ﷺ) said,

> Every deed of the son of Adam is multiplied, a single deed as ten times the like of it up to seven hundred times. Allah Almighty said, 'Except for fasting, as it is for Me and I will reward it. He leaves his desires and his food for My sake.'

Bukhari and Muslim

Amina's motivation through fasting is to be accepted as Allah's slave. After all, what is a slave? It is someone who tirelessly serves their Master. Day after day, year after year, her fasting has been consistent. She tried to hide it on many occasions but I know her so well that I realised it was just a part of her life, a part of her existence for Allah.

Many of us do not have limits and restrictions in giving sadaqa, in giving dawah (calling people to Islam), in sacrificing our sleep, and the list goes on. Amina and others like her have left their mark on me. It is never about the quantity of deeds but in the level of purity and sincerity of our deeds, as is shown in the hadith,

Verily, Allah does not look at your appearance or
wealth, but rather He looks at your hearts and actions.

Muslim

On this journey of taqwa, one of the ways to prove you are
conscious of Allah is by engaging in secret good deeds. Think
about it – if no human being knows about your actions, who
else can it ever be for? It can never be for others, as they are
completely removed from the equation. It is not to show off. It
is not to gain fame. It is not to receive something in return. It is
purely because you know Allah sees you and sees what you are
doing for Him Alone. These private deeds are the best deeds.
And they need not be big. The Messenger of Allah (ﷺ) said,

Take up good deeds only as much as you are able, for the
best deeds are those done regularly even if they are few.

Sunan Ibn Majah

There are so many distractions on this journey of taqwa – people,
progressing though life, earning a living, trials and tests, social
media – but private deeds offered consistently will keep you on
the taqwa track to Allah. Pushing yourself to do them after
establishing your salah as a priority will keep you firm – walking
and moving towards your Lord every day. Be like Amina, look
at your circumstances and keep evaluating your circumstances
as they change.

As I write this chapter, my daughter is in the thick of her final
year of completing A-Levels in Maths, Physics and Chemistry.
She is completely overwhelmed with the amount of study along-
side preparing to submit her UCAS application. It means that she
cannot observe her normal Qur'an revision portion and so commits to a smaller amount as consistently as she can. Once her
exams are over, she can up the game again. Similarly, when my
children were little and my days involved back-to-back caring

for them, the deeds I engaged in had to be ones that required less mental time – a giving of sadaqa, a smile.

I have noticed something about the more mature brothers and sisters who have reached a certain age in life. Their lives are now quieter and slower so they seem to offer more nawaafil prayer. Now this is not to say when you are young you cannot choose to offer nawaafil salah or when you are old, you cannot choose to give sadaqa. Essentially what I am saying here is, choose a good deed to be consistent upon, one that is private – between you and Allah – and choose well, based on your unique circumstances. Keep evaluating as your circumstances change.

There are three secret acts of worship that I invite you to initiate a daily practice of for the rest of your life. Yes, for the rest of your life!

They are simple and yet so profound in attaching your heart to its journey towards Allah. Here they are.

Qur'anic Reflection

Start your day contemplating the Words of your Lord as is recommended by Allah:

This is a Book that We sent down to you, a blessed Book, so people might think about its message, and the intelligent might pay attention.

Surah Sad 38:29

Again, depending on your circumstances, this may be a few lines or a page. And if you choose a few lines, it does not need to be a few lines for the rest of your life! Remember, we leave perfection to Allah.

With your daily Qur'an portion, ask yourself the following questions:

1. While I am reading the Direct Words of the Lord of the Heavens and Earth, what am I being asked to do?

   What am I being asked not to do?

2. Within these verses what can I praise Allah for?

   What can I ask Him for? (Go ahead. Pause and do those things.)

3. Today as I read these verses, what is the direct message for me?

4. What is the one action I can take today to bring these verses to life in my life?

Aiding others

As you go about your day, find ways to aid others. And do not belittle even the tiniest act of kindness and help.

> Abu Barzah reported: I said, 'O Prophet of Allah, teach me something that will benefit me.' The Prophet (ﷺ) said, 'Remove harmful things from the roads of the Muslims.'
>
> Muslim

Hold open a door for someone and let your heart tell Allah, 'This is for You.' Tell a bus driver to wait for the man running for the bus and whisper to Allah, 'This is for You.' Call a friend who is going through a rough time and offer comfort and tell your Lord, 'This is for You.'

The Messenger of Allah (ﷺ) said,

> Allah Almighty will say on the Day of Resurrection: O
> son of Adam, I was sick but you did not visit Me. He
> will say: My Lord, how can I visit You when You are the
> Lord of the Worlds? Allah will say: Did you not know
> that My servant was sick and you did not visit him, and
> had you visited him you would have found Me with
> him? O son of Adam, I asked you for food but you did
> not feed Me. He will say: My Lord, how can I feed You
> when You are the Lord of the Worlds? Allah will say: Did
> you not know that My servant asked you for food but
> you did not feed him, and had you fed him you would
> have found Me with him? O son of Adam, I asked you
> for a drink but you did not provide for Me. He will say:
> My Lord, how can I give You a drink when You are the
> Lord of the Worlds? Allah will say: My servant asked you
> for a drink but you did not provide for him, and had you
> given it to him you would have found Me with him.

Muslim

He (ﷺ) also said,

> The most beloved people to Allah are those who are most
> beneficial to people. The most beloved deed to Allah is to
> make a Muslim happy, or to remove one of his troubles,
> or to forgive his debt, or to feed his hunger. That I walk
> with a brother regarding a need is more beloved to me
> than that I seclude myself in this mosque in Medina for a
> month. Whoever swallows his anger, then Allah will
> conceal his faults. Whoever suppresses his rage, even
> though he could fulfil his anger if he wished, then Allah
> will secure his heart on the Day of Resurrection. Whoever
> walks with his brother regarding a need until he secures it

for him, then Allah Almighty will make his footing firm
across the bridge on the day when the footings are shaken.

Al-Tabaraani, *Al-Mu'jam al-Awsat*

By doing these actions for people but keeping the reason
between you and Allah, you will – by His Permission – find
yourself elevated on the Best of Days. As if this is not enough of
a reward, Ibn al-Qayyim beautifully explains,

> Perhaps you might be asleep while the doors of Heaven
> are knocking with tens of supplications for you, by a
> poor person you aided or a sad person you cheered up
> or a distressed person you brought relief to. Therefore,
> do not underestimate doing good at all.

Journal of accountability

Umar ibn al-Khattab (may Allah be pleased with him) said,

> Hold yourselves accountable before you are held
> accountable and evaluate yourselves before you are
> evaluated, for the Reckoning will be easier upon you
> tomorrow if you hold yourselves accountable today.

Ibn Abi Ad-dunya, *Muḥaasabat al-Nafs*

Keep a journal of accountability. A few lines every night is suffi-
cient and answer honestly, with no one apart from Allah knowing
what you pen:

1. How am I feeling?

2. If I am unhappy with this, what can I do to change that
tomorrow?

3. What do I need to do to become a better servant tomorrow?

If you can engage in all three, you will have learnt from Allah, acted for Allah and assessed yourself for a better tomorrow.

Returning back to Amina, she taught me an incredible lesson. We must live life on this journey of taqwa to become students of all people. Stand before everyone and everything as a student with a life lesson to take from them. Amina taught me to choose an act of ibadah, and to do it as secretly as possible, give it my all and excel in it.

Dear reader, I invite you to do the same. And maybe just maybe the angels will boast about us and say, 'That servant of Allah. That Muslim who adored Allah. In the dunya, he or she is the one that used to . . .'

Hide your good deeds as much as possible. They are for Allah, so keep them for Allah.

Let Your Heart Ponder . . .

'The Messenger of Allah (ﷺ) said, "Verily, Allah loves a servant who is righteous, independent, and obscure."'

Muslim

'O Allah, make the Qur'an the spring of my heart, the illumination of my chest, the assuaging of my grief, and the departure of my anxiety.'

Musnad Aḥmad

'I do not count actions that I do openly.'

Sufyan al-Thawri, *Sayd Al-Khater*

Du'a Invitation

Al-Ghani, The Self-Sufficient, The Rich, on this journey to You, I need to and want to offer You the best of myself and the best of my deeds. There is so much that interferes with what I do – my ego, to be seen by others, to be recognised by others. All of this will not avail me in my grave. I ask you, ya Rabbi, to occupy my concern with Your perception of me and my deeds. Make me one who proves my servitude to You by doing the very things that you love – unknown to any of your creation except your angels. Fill my scales with secret deeds that outweigh my public deeds. Make my yearning for You supersede all other yearnings. Ya Rabbi, accept my private good deeds as proof of that.

Journal

1. On this journey of taqwa, I choose to engage in the following small private deeds as consistently as I can . . .

....

....

2. Buy yourself a journal for your Qur'anic reflections. On the first page write down all the intentions you can have as you commit to this practice.

....

....

3. Who is in need of help right now? Write down his or her name.

....

....

4. How can you assist this person purely for the sake of Allah? Write it down. Now tell Allah, 'This is for You.'

....

....

5. Begin your practice of accountability. Answer the three questions from earlier in this chapter.

....

....

My reflections
on the topic of
Private Deeds are . . .

DAY 29

Was, Am or Will be Tested

'I have a feeling something is coming,' I told my friend Zainab as she dunked a chocolate digestive biscuit in her milky tea.

Zainab looked up at me and put her hand to her head. 'Don't say that, Aliyah! I don't think I can handle you going through another test.'

'I know, but I just can't shake off this feeling – things have been really good for a while, Alhamdulillah. I feel like a test is coming.'

Shortly after this, I was presented with one of the greatest trials I have ever experienced to date. This test spanned more than two years of pain and agony the like of which I pray Allah never ever tests me with again. But if He does, I know that He will always be my support.

We are all in one of three states: we were tested, are being tested or will be tested. This is the nature of this life. Allah says,

Do people think they will be left alone because they say, 'We believe', then will not be tested? We tested those before them. Allah knows the truthful and the liars.

Surah Ankabut 29:2–3

This journey of taqwa – God-consciousness – changes you. It changes what your senses take in. It changes your mind and the thoughts that roam therein. It changes your heart and softens it for Allah and all that He Loves. It changes your character, your speech and your actions. It literally changes the direction you were heading in to the one you need to travel. It changes your faith and it changes your soul.

These changes lead to a different standing with Allah whereby you become His beloved. And when Allah loves His servant, He wants His servant close to Him. He wants to purify His servant. He wants to forgive His servant and He wants His servant to be rewarded with eternal bliss and peace.

And so, He puts us to trial – not to hurt us but to draw us back to Him, to bring us back to the path when we sometimes lose our way. You see, tests, the really difficult ones, force us to turn back to Him in ways that we do not in times of ease. The forehead touches the floor again. There is an increase in the movement of one's lips as they utter desperate cries of help to Allah repeatedly. Deep internal dependency is experienced like an open, honest and deep wound. Our tests bring us back to our journey to Him.

Ibn al-Qayyim says,

> Were it not that Allah treats His slaves with the remedy of trials and calamities, they would transgress and overstep the mark. When Allah wills good for His slaves, He gives him the medicine of calamities and trials according to his situation, so as to cure him from all fatal illnesses and diseases, until He purifies and cleanses him, and then makes him qualified for the most honourable position in this world, which is that of being a true slave of Allah, and for the greatest reward in the Hereafter, which is that of seeing Him and being close to Him.

> *Zaad al-Ma'ad*

Signing up to faith, whether that is as a revert or as one born into the faith who decides to start practising, means you sign up to being tested. And the more focused you are upon the path of taqwa, the more attached you are to Allah and His Pleasure, the more you will be tested.

There is a weak hadith (i.e. weak in its chain of narration) that many scholars such as Ibn Taymiyyah (may Allah be pleased with him) have used for its wisdom. It reads,

> From amongst My servants are those whose faith would not be rectified except through poverty, and if I opened the door of wealth for him, it would corrupt him.
>
> And there are amongst My servants those whose faith would not be rectified except through wealth, and if I deprived him, it would corrupt him.
>
> And there are amongst My servants, those whose faith would not be rectified except through good health, and if I made him sick, it would corrupt him.
>
> And there are amongst My servants those whose faith would not be rectified except through illness, and if I healed him, it would corrupt him.
>
> And there are amongst My loving servants those that seek a particular station, and they have been unable to achieve it, so that they do not become conceited.
>
> I plan for My servants with My Knowledge of what is in their hearts. Verily I am All-Knowing and I am All-Aware.
>
> Omar Suleiman, *Judgement Day*, YouTube series

Part of being akhirah-focused is being aware that the journey to Allah is full of stations – Reflection, Love, Fear, Hope, Tawbah,

Gratitude, Acceptance, Tawakkul, Ihsaan and more. In between these stations we will be tested in order to receive lessons and grow before moving onto the next station on this most blessed journey. It cannot be avoided. It is a natural part of the cycle of this life.

And the beautiful thing is that we are all part of an intricate network. Our tests touch one another in various ways. The test that I endure may create an opening for another person to gain their reward. Your test and how you manage it may also be a lesson for someone else who will happen to endure it in the future.

Here we are, Day 29 of Ramadan. It has certainly been a journey – Ramadan always is. This life is like Ramadan. We pass through it so quickly. And it ends so suddenly. The end of Ramadan is met with a mixture of sadness at its departure but also happiness at the arrival of Eid-Ul-Fitr. Just as the believer, upon entering the next life, feels a sadness he or she cannot do more good deeds in the dunya but yearns to be with Allah in Jannah.

And if we are blessed with Jannah then,

> How strange does it seem, that these tests which weigh a ton on our chest today will one day elevate us. Elevate us so high, that we will thank Allah. We will thank Him for testing us, for loving us and for giving us more than anyone could imagine.

> Ibn al-Qayyim, *Al Fawaa'id*

As you move forward into your akhirah-focused future, remember this: sometimes Allah will bring about an experience that breaks your heart in order to sharpen your vision for the rest of the journey ahead.

I entrust my future to You.

Let Your Heart Ponder . . .

'The Messenger of Allah (ﷺ) said, "Verily, a man may have a rank with Allah that he does not achieve by his good deeds. Thus, Allah continues to put him to trial with what he hates until he reaches the rank destined for him."'

Ibn Ḥibban

Du'a Invitation

Ya Allah, I accept that my life moving forward will be full of tests. I know that this is to teach me, to purify me and to draw my heart towards You. I surrender to the tests You know will do all this and more. I do not question because I know You are a Compassionate, Loving and Merciful Lord. My Lord, I am human. And when it hurts, I ask You to strengthen me and carry me. In the words of Your Prophet (ﷺ), I ask You . . .

Oh Allah, I hope for Your Mercy. Do not leave me to myself even for the blinking of an eye. Correct all of my affairs for me. There is none worthy of worship but You.

Sunan Abu Dawud

Journal

1. I have used the following tools in the past which have helped me manage difficult times . . .

....

....

....

....

2. The ones that really worked for me were . . .

....

....

....

....

3. With all the topics presented in this book, how do you feel you can better manage the tests of your future?

....

....

....

....

**My reflections
on the topic of
Being Tested are . . .**

DAY 30

Allah, I Need to Talk to You about My Future

Writing this book has been an interesting experience for me. I began it feeling like I was simply not a good enough writer. I began to feel like an imposter. I was nervous and afraid that I would not do this book justice. I still do not know if I have.

There have been days where my words have flowed onto the page. There were also days where I simply stared at my laptop, completely blocked. I had to make room in my life to write this book. I enlisted the help of my loved ones to make this happen.

This book was my dream. It is the answer of a du'a I have been making for years and Allah answered it in the best of ways.

With everything I have read, every chapter I have ruminated over, every letter and word I have typed – I have done so with a clear vision of what I hope this book will do for you, my dear reader, in the future. Your future. Whether that will become a reality is not down to me. It is up to Allah, Lord of the Worlds. It is with Him now.

This journey has taught me the importance of keeping your eyes fixed on the destination. In doing so, you will be grateful for the smooth parts of the journey and you will turn to Him for help with the rough parts. The drive to get to the destination of completing this book has taught me lessons in what I need to do as I end my writing and continue with my own journey to Him.

I am actually in tears as I write this. This book has been a labour of love that I pray earns me His Love. Everything we do moving forward is for that goal and that goal alone.

These last ten days of the final third of Ramadan have been future-focused and akhirah-focused. We have made plans. We have looked at what will slow us down and what will make the journey smoother and more intimate. Thirty days of healing from our past, learning to become present and planning ahead for an akhirah-focused future. May Allah accept it from all of us. Ameen.

It is time to talk to Allah.

Allah,

O Allah, You are my Lord. There is no God but You. You created me and I am Your slave, and I remain faithful to Your covenant and Your promise as much as I can. I seek refuge with You from the wrong of what I have done. I acknowledge Your favours upon me, and I admit my sins. So forgive me, for indeed none forgives sins except You.

My Lord, have mercy upon Muhammad (ﷺ) and send peace upon him.

My Beloved Master, attach every part of my being to Your Paradise. You have promised Your righteous believing servants what no eye has ever seen, what no ear has ever heard and that which no heart can ever comprehend. You are the Almighty, the All-Wise.

Ya Rabbi, grant me the confidence and wisdom to choose how I journey to You by way of my strengths and skills. Help me identify that which I can work towards that will make You Smile upon me. When You bring opportunities my way, make me grab hold of each and every one – and run with them for You and to You.

Oh Allah, when I feel like I am chained by my worries and concerns, remind me that You are here. That You are my strength when I am weak. That You can make possible that which I worry I cannot.

I place my full hope in You that You will always bring me to that which is best for me. I go into my future with hope that the deeper my connection is with You, the stronger my hope in how You will manage my affairs will be. I place my hope in You because You are the Most Compassionate, Most Merciful, Most Loving. You will never let me down. You will always hold me up.

As part of my yearning to be beloved to You, I prioritise the importance of my communication with You. When I speak to You, I do so with certainty that You hear me. When I complain to You, I do so knowing You will comfort me. When I ask of You, I know You will grant me my du'a. I speak to You with certainty for You are a Lord who never breaks His Promises.

As-Sabur, You are Most Patient with me. Gift me with patience as I walk towards You. When I am impatient, slow me down, quieten my voice and calm my heart – remind me to turn to prayer and patience to get through.

There will be times on this journey when I need Your Help, Guidance and Direction. I place my full trust in You who possesses the keys to my future, that You will always direct me towards the best for my dunya and akhirah.

O my Beloved, before I entered the world, You took a covenant from all Your creation as proof that we testify to Your Oneness. I renew that oath. Everything aside from my private worship and devotion to You might be tainted with showing off and arrogance. In order for me to fulfil my oath with You, I ask You to bless me with many opportunities to engage in private good deeds that are only for You.

O Knower of the Future, I am committed. I am here, desiring Your Love and Your Acceptance of all that I am and do for Your Sake. I ask You to grant me all that is good and when you test me, strengthen me and be with me, ya Rabbi. Keep my sight focused on the destination ahead.

You are my Creator and Master. Forgive me for my past, bless me in my present and keep me focused on my future. You are a Lord who is Just. Grant me balance in all the seasons of my life.

Go back to the reflections on the topics that you journaled about at the end of the previous nine chapters. Read over them. Now pen your own private thoughts about your akhirah-focused future, to the One who Knows what is to come and the One who will be with you every step of the way.

Glossary

Abaya: Islamic dress
Adhaan: Call to prayer
Adhkaar: Morning and evening prayer and remembrance
Ahadith qudsi: Allah's Words as shared by the Prophet (ﷺ)
Akhirah: Eternal life
Alhamdulillah: All praise and thanks are due to Allah
Allahu akbar: Allah is Greater than everything
Amanah: Upholding of trust
Assalamu alaikum: Peace be upon you
Awliya: Close friend
Ayah: Verse
'azza wa jal: Glory be to Him
Barakah: Blessings
Bi'idhnillah: By Allah's Permission
Bismillah: In the name of Allah
Dawah: Calling people to Islam
Deen: Way of life
Dhikr: Remembrances of Allah
Du'a: Personal prayer of supplication
Dunya: This life
Faraa'id: Obligatory acts of worship
Firdous al ala: Highest level of Paradise
Haram: Prohibited
Hifdh: Memorisation
Hijrah: Emigration to a Muslim country
Ibadah: Worship
Iftar: Post-dusk meal

Ihsaan: The state of worshipping Allah as though you see Him and though you cannot see Him, knowing He sees you

Imaan: Faith

Insha'Allah: God willing

Istighfaar: The act of seeking forgiveness from Allah

Jannah: Paradise

Jumu'ah: Friday sermon and prayer

Khawf: Fear

Khushoo: Focus in prayer

La hawla wa la quwwata illa billah: There is no Power or Might except with Allah

Laylatul Qadr: The Night of Decree

Masjid: mosque

Muhsin: One who aims to achieve the state of ihsaan

Muhsineen: People who aim to achieve the state of ihsaan

Mu'min: One who submits in action and becomes a true believer in faith

Muttaqeen: Believers who are ever conscious of Allah

Nafs: Ego

Naseeha: Advice

Nawaafil: Recommended acts of worship

Qadr: Divine Decree

Rabbi: My Lord

Raka'at: Two units of prayer

Ramadan: The ninth month in the Islamic calendar where fasting is prescribed

Riyaa: Pride

Sabrun jameel: A beautiful patience

Sadaqa: Charity

Sadaqa jariah: Charity that continues after death

Salah: Prayer

Salatul istikharaa: The prayer for guidance

Salawaat: Peace and blessings on the Prophet (ﷺ)

Seerah: Life of the Prophet

Shahaadah: Declaration of faith

Subhana'Allah: How free of any imperfection is Allah
Subhanahu wa ta'ala (سبحانه وتعالى): Glorious and Most High is He
Suhoor: Pre-dawn meal
Sunnah: Tradition
Tahajjud: Prayer at the last part of the night
Taqwa: God-consciousness
Taraweeh: Ramadan prayer
Tawakkul: Full reliance upon Allah
Tawbah: The return to Allah through repentance
Ubudiyyah: Servitude
Wudu: Ablution before prayer
Yaqeen: Certainty

Select Bibliography

Where publication or edition details have not been listed, the English translations in the text have been provided by independent translators.

Abdullah, B. B. *Timeless Seeds of Advice,* independently published, 2019

Abdullah al-Asfahani, Ahmad bin, *Ḥilyat al-Awliyā'*

Abdur-Razzaq bin Abdul-Muhsin al-Badr, *Hifdh al-Waqt fi Ramadan*

Al-Bayhaqi, *Kitab Fada'il al-Awqat*

Al-Tabaraani, *Al-Mu'jam al-Awsat*

Bridges' Translation of the Ten Qira'At of the Noble Qur'An, tr. Fadel Soliman, Authorhouse, 2020

Hussain, Musharraf, *The Majestic Quran,* Invitation Publishing, 2019, 2nd edition

Ibn Abi Ad-dunya, *Muḥaasabat al-Nafs*

Ibn Baz, *Hadeeth al-Masaa'*

Ibn al-Jawzi, *Sayd Al-Khater*
——, *Aqwal Ibn al-Jawzi*
——, *Kitab Al-Lataif*
——, *Sifat as Safwah*

Ibn al-Qayyim, *Al-Fawaa'id*
—, *Haadi al-Arwaah ilaa Bilaad il-Afraah*
—, *Ighathat al-Lahfan*
—, *Madaarij As-Salikeen*
—, *Zaad al-Ma'ad*

Jangda, Abdul Nasir, 'Istikharaa: how to and why', Muslim Matters website, 13 Jan 2020. Available at: https://muslimmatters. org/2012/01/13/abdul-nasir-jangda-istikharah- how-to-and-why-2/

Suleiman, Omar, *Judgement Day: Deeds that Light the Way*, podcast series, Yaqeen Institute for Islamic Research, YouTube, 2022

Gratitude

This book has been a labour of love and I feel so very emotional as I pen this final page of thanks.

I start where gratitude is always due first – with my Lord, Allah. This book came from You, ya Rabbi and it is for You. I feel honoured and humbled that You answered my du'a: to write and publish a book before I leave this world. All praise and thanks is due to You. Guide me to remember that everything is only because You permitted it. Guide me to always be grateful for all of Your Blessings upon me. Ameen.

I would like to thank my publisher, Olivia Morris. Olivia, thank you for following your instinct and taking a chance on an unknown author and sending that DM! Lots of thanks must go to my dear sister in faith, Na'ima B. Robert, who was one of the first to find out about this book and introduced me to my fabulous agent, Sheri Safran. Na'ima, in that one simple act, you embodied the hadith 'Love for your fellow Muslim, what you love for yourself.' May Allah love you. Ameen.

My New Yorker agent, Sheri, you've been an absolute boss and there is no way I could have navigated this process without you. I've grown so fond of you and couldn't have asked for a better agent.

Sue Lascelles, my dear editor, I thank you for your patience, kindness and reassurance along this journey, as well as the few laughs we've had along the way! I have thoroughly enjoyed working with you.

Special thanks must go to Danai Denga, assistant editor at PRH. Danai, you have blown me away with the beautiful way you have interacted with me; taking in my opinions and always sending emails that are infused with respect, kindness and understanding.

Thank you to LaYinka Sanni – grateful for your love and the dinner treat, wherein you pointed out the blurb had to change!

Thank you to Cherr Madayag. Cherr, you patiently reviewed cover draft after cover draft. May Allah always bless your visionary skills. Ameen.

Farhia Yahya – you did it again, girlfriend! You came up with the name Solace and now the cover image of this book. Allah always sends you to me at the right time.

Now on to the following people who, when I think about them, my eyes fill with tears. This book would not have been possible without them. First is my beautiful long-term friend Hajar who cooked for my family during the final week of my writing month and popped over with a bottle of halal 'champagne' and chocolates on the day I was due to submit my manuscript. Hajar, you stayed up with me until midnight, waiting to celebrate once I had hit the send button. Hajar, I love you beyond words and appreciate you more than you can ever imagine.

To my colleagues at Solace, especially Najat and Urwah, who took on some of my work tasks and displayed so much patience as I completed this book. You are not just colleagues. You are my family. I appreciate you all.

To the mothers of my youngest daughter's friends who helped me, Sarah, Karina and Aaliyah, sometimes without knowing how much they helped me. May Allah love you and your families. Ameen.

To Ruji Rahman, who patiently gave me dawah all those years ago – may this book weigh heavily on your scales. Ameen.

And now the biggest thanks of all go to my beautiful family. Words cannot express what you all mean to me. Throughout this entire process, you have been extremely patient with me. When I cried out of exhaustion, you told me, 'Come on! You can do this!' When I was repeatedly unavailable, you didn't complain. You understood, supported me, encouraged me, believed in me and willed me on to the finish line. You are my constants. You have shown me true love. I love you all so very much. Without your patience and support, this book would not have been possible. May Allah love and guide you always. Ameen.

I end, thanking Allah again. He is the First and the Last. Gratitude to the people is gratitude to Him, for the people who have been a part of this journey were placed perfectly by Him. True gratitude is realising everything must always be attributed to Him. My life and my dreams are only by His Will, His Generosity and His Mercy.

Allah, I ask You to accept this little deed of mine and to forgive me for any shortcomings therein.

About the Author

Aliyah Umm Raiyaan reverted to Islam in 1999 as a young woman and has been involved in UK dawah for over twenty years. In 2010, she founded Solace UK, a charity that helps women who have reverted to Islam and find themselves in difficulty. In 2019, she launched a YouTube show called *Honest Tea Talk*, which brought unscripted conversations to the table about raw unspoken topics related to the Muslim community. She continues to devote her time to helping women achieve their full potential whilst emphasising the importance of developing a personal and close relationship with Allah. She lives in East London with her family.